CORPORATE
MADNESS

How to Change the System When the System Refuses to Change

By
William D. Stinnett, Ph.D.
and
Russell G. Hanson, M.S.E.

LEADERSHIP PRESS

The excerpt on page 17 is from "Miles to Go...or Unity at Last," by Brian Usilaner and John Leitch, *Journal for Quality and Participation*, June 1989. Reprinted with permission.

The excerpt on page 165 is from *A Passion for Excellence*, by Tom Peters and Nancy Austin, Random House Inc., New York, NY, 1985. Reprinted with permission.

10   9   8   7   6   5   4   3   2   1

This edition published by Leadership Press, 124 W. Orion, Suite F-10, Tempe AZ 85283, (602) 730-1752.

Printed in the United States of America.

Library of Congress Cataloging in Publication Data
Stinnett, William D.
Hanson, Russell G.
    Corporate madness, How to change the system when the system refuses to change
    Includes bibliographic references, glossary, and index
Business
I. Title
HF5001   658.46   90-60205

Library of Congress Catalog Card No. 90-60205
ISBN: 0-9625630-0-5

We Dedicate This Book
to Robin and Margie

TABLE OF CONTENTS

PREFACE

Trying to improve organizational performance is nothing new. Whether motivated by competitive spirit, entrepreneurial zeal, greed, or patriotism, countless attempts have been made to achieve the pinnacle of performance.

Ever since the turn of the century when Americans became infatuated with technology and its promise for a higher quality of life, people have sought ways to improve productivity. From Frederic W. Taylor, who saw the organization as a machine, through the traditional top-down hierarchy and the innovative bottom-up concept of quality circles, professionals have pursued "The Answer." Past approaches have identified many sound ideas for productivity improvement. The ability to recognize valid information and adjust, the importance of participation, prevention versus inspection, accountability, incremental improvement, process orientation, a systems viewpoint, and many other principles constitute the cornerstone of many successful improvement efforts.

Where we diverge from the other concepts is in the method of execution. As with any good idea, the effect is only as good as its execution. The approach we advocate, which we call Total Employee Involvement (TEI), greatly enhances the probability that the change will be fully adopted, made to stick, and actually produce the desired results. Perhaps TEI is simply a higher evolution of these other concepts, but we can attest to the success of these methods, as can the thousands of workers and managers who use them every day.

Needless to say, we did not arrive at these solutions by ourselves. Many people helped along the way and we'd like to recognize them in some small way for their very significant contributions. Much of the credit for the ideas in this book and indeed the successes we have seen and read about goes to organizational improvement practitioners from our not too distant past. A few who come immediately to mind are Frederick Hertzberg, Rensis Likert, Kurt Lewin, Abraham Maslow, and Douglas McGregor. Additional credit is certainly due to Chris Argyris, W. Edwards Deming, Robert Cole, Joseph Juran, W.S. Rieker, Thomas Gordon, Tom Peters, Warren Bennis, and many others. Each of these people clearly saw deficiencies in corporate methodology and each had a vision of how such enterprise could be conducted more productively and humanely.

On a more immediate level are the people who have contributed personally to this effort. Bill Van Horn, who worked with us in our initial project, had had previous successes in employee involvement programs. We believe the term "Total Employee Involvement" and its key elements—the inclusion of all members of the work unit in the process from its inception, defining the work unit as a business-within-a-business, and defining success as meeting the needs of the business and the needs of the people—are the invention of Bill Van Horn, who became our manager and mentor in 1980. We thank Bill for his vision, his guidance, and his generosity.

We also wish to thank a few of our many colleagues, clients, and friends who have contributed their ideas, talent, and enthusiasm to the implementation and development of the concepts in this book:

Frank Applegate
Kathy Bates
Steve Borstleman
Jerry Buldoc
Larry Burr
Dale Canady
Fred Cheyunski
Dick Cogan
Jeff Crouch
Roy Dawson
Mary Anne Donahue
Mike Donovan
Ted Edwards
Wally Estfan
Pat Hesselman
Louise Holloway
Will Jones
Chet Kenrich
Les Killingsworth
Mike Killion
Arthur Lloyd
Bob Marki
George McNeil
Judi Neal-Stach
Julie Nelson
Peter Newell
Kathy Parker
Norm Perrill
Alan Price
Doug Reid
Al Van Arsdal
Jim Widfelt
Melanie Young

We also offer a special word of thanks to Maureen Norris, Project Manager for the book, and Mary Westheimer, our editor, for holding our feet to the fire to complete the manuscript and leading us through the maze of production.

And last but hardly least, we thank the corporate leaders who understood the mission and its rewards and accepted the challenge, and the thousands of employees who have embraced Total Employee Involvement and through it found fulfillment in their jobs.

INTRODUCTION

THE NATURE OF MADNESS

Although the past often seems rosier in retrospect, there are memories that shine brilliantly in every past. During and shortly after the second world war, U.S. industrialists enjoyed true halcyon years. Yes, the war was looming or already underway and shortages stymied supplies, but demand seemed insatiable and workers indefatigably dedicated. In that period, American industrialists developed a remarkable ability to produce and deliver a staggering array of goods and services. This period created an affluent standard of living unmatched by any society at any time in the history of the world before or since. While the resulting prosperity was certainly a noble achievement, today we are facing that era's grim and unintentional consequences.

Confronted with little competition and a hungry marketplace, success came easily. Managers didn't have to do things well to make money, and the environment was extremely fertile for the development of bad habits. And develop they did. For the most part, managers stumbled through their field of duties, maintaining the pace simply because demand insisted upon forward progress. If they did learn about working with employees and developing effective systems, much of that learning was accidental. Managers developed new management techniques, but these actions often had no real connection to their achievements. Psychologists call this sort of accidental learning, the kind used by the gambler who blows on his dice or wears his lucky hat, superstitious behavior.

Because of their success, these behaviors were passed on from generation to generation, and a disturbing number survive today. The problem, of course, is that today's world is very different from that heady heyday. Today's managers are confronted with tremendous competition, demanding, sophisticated and wary customers, and employees who are much more likely to challenge managerial authority. Nonetheless, managers cling to these superstitious behaviors. Their persistence isn't entirely unforgivable—after all, it's much easier to recognize faults in others that are all but invisible in yourself.

So, in the face of overwhelming evidence to the contrary, managers continue to solve quality lapses by adding more inspectors, respond to schedule difficulties by speeding up production lines, react to cost quandaries by laying off employees and cutting back on research and education, and trying to solve performance problems by threatening and punishing employees. This, we believe, is madness.

WHY MADNESS?

The dictionary gives five definitions of madness:

> (1) Dementia; insanity; lunacy. (2) Great anger; fury. (3) Great folly. (4) Wild excitement or enthusiasm. (5) Rabies.

While there may be cases of insanity—or even rabies—in the American workplace, the purpose of this book is to explore the meaning of definitions 2, 3, and 4. Every day, thousands of workers, whether white or blue collar, express their anger. It is often smoldering and persistent and directed at the system or management or at "some people around here," but with no clear target nor any effective release. Such anger is universal in the workplace and it is fueled by folly.

Changing the way business is done requires a madness of a different sort. Wild excitement or enthusiasm and perhaps a touch of recklessness may be an apt description of the characteristics needed to make the change, but we'll get to that later.

FURY AND FOLLY

During our work with major corporations, we often confront a stunning paradox in both employee and manager responses. Almost everyone queried laments, "I work my fingers to the bone because I care about what happens around here, but nobody else gives a damn." They often continue, "I feel all alone. I feel like giving up." Or, even worse, they reveal, "I've given up. Not because I don't care, but no one else seems to care and I finally just got tired."

The truly remarkable thing about these responses is that they create an unbelievable situation. It simply isn't possible that everyone cares yet everyone around them doesn't. Either everyone is lying, which seems unlikely, or there is a sort of madness, a hysteria, created by the very way we conduct business that causes such feelings and such a distorted view of the situation.

Since the overwhelming majority of these employees and managers are individuals of exceedingly high decency, honesty, and integrity, madness seems a more likely explanation.

Fury and folly rears its head in many forms. There is no clearer way to illustrate corporate madness than the following anecdotes.

> A manufacturer that supplies large government contractors requires seven to twelve managers review and sign change orders. In actuality, however, on the average only two of the people in the signature cycle even read the document. **Madness masquerading as accountability.**

> Pressed to meet a delivery schedule, a production manager delivers a sham device to a customer. After allowing the customer to complain for several weeks that the fake device is not working, the manager, who by this time has the actual device working, clandestinely substitutes the real thing. **Madness passing for on-time delivery.**

> A successful employee involvement process at a circuit board factory produces a 140 percent gain in productivity in a single year. Senior management reasons that the plant manager and his employees must have been "sandbagging" before. They fire the plant manager and lay off 15 percent of the workforce. **Madness disguised as cost reduction.**

> A manufacturer of a home electronics product is having serious quality problems. Huge queues are causing delays in produc-

tion and adding to the original quality problems and the floor is cluttered with reworked and returned product. With the work area so crowded, management decides it has a "space problem." The solution? Build a new warehouse and install a gigantic conveyor from the factory so returned product and product needing rework can be removed from the factory. They reason that, if they can get the bad product out of the way, they can eliminate delays, keep production going and meet their schedules. The result? The quality problems continue and the new warehouse fills up with bad product. The financial losses become so high that the company has to close its doors and sell the business. The Japanese company that purchases it removes the conveyor, solves the quality problems, and makes a profit in the first twelve months of operation. **Madness rationalized as devotion to the production schedule.**

A customer service department at a major utility company is plagued with complaints about poor service. Management reasons that the customer service representatives must be goofing off. The solution? They install a system that monitors the amount of time each terminal is in use, how many times each phone rings, and how many incoming calls are lost. In addition to the monitoring, new rules require operators to remain at their terminals at all times unless they receive permission to go to the bathroom, take breaks, or go to lunch. Supervisors are expected to punish operators who fall below certain performance levels, but aren't to say anything to the operators until they are in trouble. The consequences? The best operators leave the company. Customer calls are answered, but the operators rush their responses, cut calls short, and generally are less effective in solving customers' problems. So the chaos multiplies: The frequency of calls increases and the number of customer complaints rises while customer satisfaction plummets. Costs also climb as additional operators have to be hired and trained to handle the higher volume. Management blames the new problems on employees' "bad attitude," and crack down with more supervision and stiffer penalties. The result? Even greater increases in complaints and further decreases in customer satisfaction. **Madness as tyranny instead of leadership.**

A group of test technicians at a large electronics manufacturing company complain about the time and energy wasted getting common parts for various tests. Each time one of the hundreds of tests is run, various kinds of resistors or capacitors need to be attached to the hardware before, then removed after the test. Whenever a technician needs such a part, many of which cost only pennies, he or she must request the part from a production control expeditor. The expeditor documents the request, submits it to the proper department, picks up the part from the stockroom, and delivers it to a manufacturing lead person, who assigns an assembler to attach the part to the hardware. The group leader then gives the completed hardware to the production control expeditor who delivers it to the test technician who conducts the test, then returns it to the production control expeditor who gives it to the group leader who assigns the job to an assembler who removes the part from the hardware. And if the device fails the test? You guessed it: the whole process is repeated. The technicians reason that much time and money could be saved by having technicians acquire, attach, and remove these special parts themselves. Unfortunately, a rule doesn't permit that. The waste continues. **Madness as organized procedures.**

These anecdotes are all sad but true. Communication and trust between management and workers is lost somewhere in the corporate "cold war," in which, rather than pursuing a common goal, the two groups have become adversaries.

The last sketch illustrates the beginning of the end, and a most common complaint among workers disillusioned with corporate initiatives: "We brought that up and nobody did anything about it." Convinced that they'll be ignored, scolded, or punished if they make a suggestion, employees feel little or no motivation to participate. At this stage, the crux of the problem is management credibility. **Fair or unfair, employees often simply do not believe what management tells them.** Unless this roadblock is removed, progress is unlikely. Nothing management says will do much good unless the employees believe it.

Often, managers are reluctant to accept this. About six years ago, a corporate initiative was instituted at a major manufacturing firm to spur employee participation. Typical management rhetoric included, "Tell us what you need and we'll see that you get it." The suggestions poured in. But the company wasn't prepared to respond to the recommendations and, despite good intentions, nothing happened. Soon the suggestions stopped coming. So the company began a new initiative. Rather than developing a system to respond to the suggestions, they decided to regulate them. Management told the employees, "Tell us what your problems are as long as they require no additional resources to fix them." The employees are angry, management is confused, and the suggestions have stopped coming. Big surprise!

This book, though, is not about some magical corporate world where there are no problems. Every company has problems. But what so many of them lack is an ability to understand those problems and solve them in a way that benefits not just management, not just stockholders, but everyone who comes in contact with the company, from the humblest employee to the smallest customer. We maintain that **any** company can become a place where the madness is not anger and folly, but wild excitement and enthusiasm, and we can tell you how. This approach can be used to strengthen already established improvement programs or as the framework for creating new ones.

SOME BAD NEWS

As you read, you're possibly thinking, "Sure, sure, I've heard all of this before. This is just another book about participative management and how we should get employees more involved in their work. They think they've got the magic solution that will solve all our problems." We recognize fully that there is no simple answer to today's complex business challenges. In fact, we are not attempting to provide an "answer." What we are proposing is a methodology you can use to develop the best possible solutions to your unique set of problems. However, the path is rocky, the travel treacherous, and there is no guarantee of success.

Most corporate initiatives, in fact, don't work and neither do most employee involvement programs. According to a study by A.T. Kearney (1985), although 80 percent of the Fortune 1000 firms had attempted quality circles, fully 83 percent of them abandoned the idea within eighteen months. In another study of Fortune 500 companies conducted by the U.S. General Accounting Office, Brian Usilaner and John Leitch (1989) note that, while 80 percent of all these companies report some form of employee involvement, they are not doing a very good job of it. "The bad news is that what is being done and planned is woefully inadequate...The EI approaches being implemented have little impact on an organization's decision-making process." More madness!

These conclusions are consistent with our own experiences. It appears that 80 percent of larger businesses have tried some form of employee involvement and that 80 percent of those attempts have been abandoned. Furthermore, 80 percent of those remaining have programs that have produced only a portion of the desired and expected results. This leaves a mere 4 percent that have truly made these ideas work.

Why? Because they're a bad idea? Because there's no management commitment? Not enough money being invested? While all of these factors have played some part in failed programs, by far the overwhelming spoiler is poor execution. Managers simply do not know how to execute well, and the people they hire to do it for them don't know any more than they do. It's a lot like health and fitness. You can buy exercise machines, diet books, join health spas, and go to lectures on nutrition, but unless you actually exercise and eat sensibly, none of it matters much.

It may surprise you, but we believe the approach to improvement matters little. What matters greatly is whether the management involved is willing to do what is absolutely necessary to create a process that can be built and sustained.

Employee involvement isn't an end and it isn't the result. Total Employee Involvement, the process we advocate in corporations throughout the United States and here in this book, is an ongoing, multifaceted approach that systematically involves all employees from all levels and functions within the organization in a process of continuous improvement.

The nature of these mechanisms, the inner workings of the process itself, is what this book is all about. This is not a formula. There is no formula. But if you're going to succeed, you are going to have to accept certain things. One of them is that the "Initiative of the Year" method will not work here. You know the scenario: A senior executive reads a book or attends a workshop and decides that this program is just what the company needs. He assigns a staff person to investigate it and get back to him on how to do it. The staff person reports that the program requires A, B, C, D, and E. The executive says, "I like B, C, and E, but not A and D. Go implement B, C, and E, but fire anyone who does A and D." Everyone smiles and nods their heads. Six months later it's business as usual. Then the executive reads another book and the cycle continues.

To make this work, you must execute all parts of the process, not just the ones that sound good. That is not to say you should try to do everything exactly as described in this book. If madness of the worst sort has created a monstrous crisis full of danger, fear, folly, mischief, and inexplicable paradoxes, then only madness of a different sort can bring progress. These chapters tell a story of that different sort of madness. The first chapter outlines the major events of the first year of change in a small circuit board factory in Arizona. There, the Total Employee Involvement process found its roots in a demonstration project that proved the power and potential of an entire organization focused on a vision of improved productivity and quality of worklife. Although we've changed the name to protect the innocent (and the guilty), the events we describe actually occurred and the charts represent what really happened.

Later chapters describe in more detail the day-to-day and actual nuts-and-bolts activities that made the change happen. But this story is more than a parable. We chose to describe a single organization in detail in order to give the readers practical information on **how** to proceed with a major change effort rather than describing a wide variety of efforts with superficial discussions of each. Many approaches will work when properly executed. The emphasis here is on the process and details of execution.

Every company has its own challenges, so for the process to work best for your company, you'll need to adjust it to work for you. Our model company, Finley Electronics, will provide an example, a peg on which we can hang our process' proverbial hat.

It will show you how the process works, but there will be situations where you will need to vary from Finley's approach to best fit your own company. What we offer in these chapters, however, is a guide for developing the key ingredients of a substantive, successful change, a change employees not only want, but hunger for, a change that management has begged for. For some of you, it will be the beginning of the beginning, an opportunity to create a workable system on a clean slate. For others, it will mean unknotting hard-held beliefs in promise of a brighter future for all, but either way, we assure you, it will be worth the effort.

CHAPTER ONE

A MICROCOSM OF MADNESS

IN THE BEGINNING

The tiny Finley Electronics cafeteria was crowded with people. Tables had been pushed aside and extra chairs brought in to accommodate the entire day shift. Over the hum of vending machines, the operations director began telling the group of about 120 operators, managers, supervisors, engineers, and office workers about plans for major changes in the way the company wanted to involve people in the business during the upcoming year. Part of this kick-off included the recitation of a manifesto or credo full of high-minded promises about trust, quality, teams, and commitment. He stood behind a podium and read aloud:

"Finley Manifesto

We at the Finley facility are changing the way we do business on a day-to-day basis. From now on we are going to establish the following principles as a Manifesto, or credo, which the organization will strive to uphold:

- We will establish a work environment of mutual trust and respect, with each person being a member of a team and allowed to participate in and influence the operation of the facility.

- We will strive to do things right the first time and quality work will be one of our goals. We assume that errors are avoidable and will therefore concentrate on preventing defects rather than just finding and fixing them.

- We will receive feedback about how well we are doing as individuals and as a team. We will set goals that have meaning to us.

- We will all be trained in problem-solving techniques and the teams will be devoted to analyzing and solving problems selected by the team. Presentations of the team solution will be made by the team to management.

- We will recognize that we are dedicated to a people development process and will help each other to grow. Improved productivity and quality of worklife will result as each of us becomes involved in our work in a meaningful way.

- We will obtain the tools and equipment that we agree are necessary for performing error-free work.

- We will conduct ourselves on a win-win basis. Constructive suggestions about improvement, roles or behavior will be encouraged. This does not mean we will say 'yes' to every idea, but it does mean we will listen to each other and fairly evaluate what is said."

As he read, skeptics rolled their eyes, and a few wags poked fun at potentially suggestive passages. If you listened closely, you could hear some of the employees murmur, "Well, at least we got a break in the day," and "More crap. I wonder what it'll be tomorrow." When the director finished, the room was quiet except for some polite applause and the usual impatient squirming.

What the people at that meeting didn't know, though, was that this employee involvement process wasn't going to be like any other. It wasn't a facade, it wasn't lip service. And each and every employee would eventually be a critical part of a success that would be shared time and time again in corporate America.

The story actually begins, however, several months earlier. Finley is a satellite operation of a large multinational electronics manufacturer with divisional headquarters in Phoenix, Arizona. The plant provides the internal layers of multilayer circuit boards assembled at the main factory thirty miles away.

About two years before, the main plant had tried to initiate a quality circles program they called Participative Quality Teams (PQT). An in-house facilitator was assigned to devote half his time to the project, and he began absorbing the information from every book and tape on quality circles he could get his hands on. Employees and management alike had begun with enthusiasm, but soon the program began breaking down. Team participation was strictly voluntary. Employees who didn't serve on the voluntary teams began to grouse that those on the teams were receiving special treatment. Some team members showed up regularly, but others were lax about attendance. Management had drawn a line through certain subjects—personnel issues, for instance, were off limits—and many of the problems raised got no further than being aired in a meeting. "We'd bring up the problem," explained one disappointed team member, "and then it'd get shuffled off to some executive committee and that's the last we'd hear of it." The more problems that poured into the system, the wider the cracks became.

Hip deep in problems, the facilitator realized the process was not working the way it was intended and he took this message to the operations director. Convinced that something had to be done, the director then went to his superiors. A fateful decision was made. The company decided to commit itself to success by bringing in experts from inside and outside the company and giving them the authority they needed to try a truly different approach, one that had garnered significant improvements in other organizations. Contrary to the contemporary top-down or bottom-up approaches, this effort would involve all employees in the change process.

The three experts who composed what became known as the Employee Productivity Program, or EPP, each had special qualities to offer. One man came from another section of the parent company, where he had had two previous successes using a similar approach. The second man, also from within the company, was an industrial engineer who understood the company managerially and technically, and grasped process measurement techniques, an attribute that would prove quite valuable. The third man was the outsider, just the kind that some business people dismiss with a sniff. He was a university professor with a solid background in the behavioral sciences, and the one who would help find the right "buttons" to push.

First, a nucleus group that included the EPP staff, the operations director and some other high-level managers was established. The group saw clearly that the PQT program was not viable, and they began developing a new approach they called Total Employee Involvement. As the concept evolved, the staff planned a complete transformation from the established hierarchical top-down management structure to one in which all employees would be involved in a participative, problem-solving team process. They knew that much of what they were proposing was controversial at best. Most quality circle programs—the latest wave in corporate improvement—insisted on voluntary participation, but the nucleus group had seen some of the problems that had caused. They knew, too, that they would need the unequivocal support of all management. These were big requests, but the problems they sought to erase were substantial, too.

These decisions aside, there was a lot of work to do. The first step was to choose a work unit within the plant that would serve as a living, breathing laboratory. Because this would be the first attempt at implementing such a significant change in a complete work unit, management knew it would have to choose the pilot organization carefully. The ideal unit would be small enough to manage effectively, relatively self-contained, and have a clearcut task, a reasonably stable workforce, and receptive management. It would also have enough opportunity for productivity and quality improvement that success would be apparent and measurable.

Finley was clearly the best candidate. With a fairly new and modern facility, the organization was isolated enough from the main plant so changes could be made without significantly affecting—or disrupting—the rest of the factory. Finley's workforce consisted of approximately seventy-five hourly production employees and thirty-nine supervisory, administrative, and technical support staff, most of whom, except for top-level management, had been with the company since the plant had been purchased by the corporation about a year earlier. A new plant manager had been brought in who wanted to install an employee participation process, but didn't really know how to go about it. Finally, because the new circuit boards the group produced were much more complex than those manufactured before, the factory was suffering from major production and quality problems. Finley was made-to-order for a microcosmic test run on the new concept, and management agreed to let the EPP staff proceed with the implementation.

Once again, however, there was some groundwork to be done. In mid-February 1981, an attitude survey was administered to all Finley personnel to establish a baseline measure of employees' perceptions about the effectiveness of the employee involvement process. It would be administered periodically to occasionally judge participants' changing attitudes and perceptions. This measurement tool would prove invaluable as the process evolved. "It allowed us to always be able to compare our current situation with the original one, but also helped us keep a realistic perspective of the employees' viewpoint throughout," a staff member would later comment. "It is a critical part of the process." A week later, the all-employee kickoff meetings were held on each of the two shifts. It was here that management members voiced their commitment to the Finley Manifesto and the staff outlined how the team process would function and what each member's role would be.

The employees' reactions, though, were quite predictable and not nearly so enthusiastic. During the presentation and the question-and-answer period that followed, people were quiet and unresponsive. The few questions asked indicated sullen resistance to the EI process. At one point, a tall, husky man from the copper plating line leaned forward in his chair and, with a sneer, asked, "Is this team stuff gonna make the dudes that screw off around here all day get off their rear ends and start workin' for a change?" One of the clerks, a young woman who looked rather bored with the whole thing, inquired, "Is this program mandatory? What if we don't want to be on a team?"

It hadn't taken long for that question to crop up, but the staff was prepared. One of them explained, "We've looked at this process and many others. We're convinced that if we don't all participate it just won't work." Eventually they struck a bargain with the employees: participation would be mandatory, but if progress wasn't apparent within six months, the experiment would be abandoned.

Despite their agreement to continue, only a handful of people were even warily optimistic. When asked what they thought about the new approach, several replied, "Well, I hope it works like you say it will. I guess it's worth a try. We sure need to do something to improve things around here."

Management and the EPP staff weren't surprised about the response, although they had secretly hoped for more enthusiasm. What they weren't prepared for, however, was what happened after the meeting. As the staff walked back to their cars, a small group of employees approached them in the parking lot. A tall, young woman stepped forward. She quickly recounted several horror stories that painted a dismal picture of the Finley situation. She described textbook examples of authoritarian management and primitive supervisory actions, favoritism, fear tactics, and numerous cases of personal conflicts between employees, including some racial disputes. Afterward, each staff member drove home mulling serious reservations about the herculean task they'd just signed up for.

AND THEY'RE OFF

The week after the kickoff meeting, the entire workforce—from the production operators to the plant manager—was formed into twelve employee involvement teams. Each of the eight production teams consisted of six to ten operators from a given work area, the production and/or quality engineer who supported that part of the factory, and the area supervisor, who served as team leader. In addition, there was a maintenance team, an engineering team, and an office support team. The last group evolved from the nucleus group. It was called the bridge team and consisted of all Finley managers, the EPP staff, and representatives from the finance and employee relations departments, with the plant manager as the team leader. Each team was facilitated by one of the EPP staff.

At each team's first meeting, the team members got to know one another better and learned more about the employee involvement process. They then learned about brainstorming and how it generates a large volume of ideas from a small group. The teams tackled two basic questions:

- How can we be more productive?

* How can we make this a better place to work?

In all, more than 450 individual ideas, issues, and problems were identified by the teams during these initial brainstorming sessions. At first the sheer number seemed daunting. The one member of the EPP staff who had experienced this before pointed out, however, that the number accounted for about five problems per person. The staff relaxed a bit, but the management couldn't help but reveal a creeping terror. Now a critical point had arrived. All eyes focused on management to see how it would respond to the teams' needs and requests.

The bridge team quickly sorted through the suggestions and began immediately addressing as many as possible. Many of them concerned basic hygiene and work setting issues: restroom cleanliness, cafeteria food quality, getting a phone line installed in one of the work areas, ordering new shop coats. Management responded swiftly and positively, implementing many suggestions within the first two weeks and communicating their actions to the teams. The message was clear: They were listening and acting promptly. This was not just lip service.

That's not to say the initial few weeks of implementation were easy for management. It was an extremely trying and frustrating period for the bridge team. Not only did they have several hundred issues demanding their attention, but many of the ideas seemed rather petty and had nothing to do with productivity or quality. The managers didn't want to waste valuable time addressing problems that had no direct impact on the product.

Their reaction, however, was normal in an environment characterized by low trust between management and workers. The hygiene issues were really a test of management's commitment to the process and sincerity in addressing the people's needs, real or perceived. **Only when management passes this "test of faith" by treating all issues as legitimate, will workers respond by addressing the needs of the business such as productivity and quality.** Fortunately, the managers gritted their teeth and dedicated themselves to the task. They had passed their first "test."

At the same time, each team began prioritizing the problems they'd raised and selecting the ones they would tackle as a team, the ones they'd send on to the bridge team, and those they'd work on individually. Slowly, enthusiasm began to build as people saw the bridge team respond. Perhaps, they realized, they could now have some influence in the factory and the operation they lived and breathed every workday. Their attention now turned to production and quality-related issues.

Some of the problems seemed quite simple, but had significant impact on the operation's productivity. One team, for instance, chose as its team project eliminating dented circuit board panels, a major cause of scrap and rework in the area. At first, team members dismissed operator handling of panels as one of the primary causes of dents. But after gathering information by observing the panels entering and leaving each operation in the area, they discovered that many of the dents were indeed due to the way the panels were handled. When the team leader asked for ideas about how to resolve the problem, one team member piped up, "Well, we'll just stop denting them." The problem disappeared almost immediately! Obviously, careful handling was a solution that had been repeatedly drilled into operators' heads by the engineers and supervisors for many months. So what was the difference this time? **The operators now felt some real ownership and responsibility for the solution of the problem.**

Other problems, however, were more complex. Another team struggled over why, in the same production run, there were many open and shorted-circuit runs on some panels and relatively few or none on others. They finally traced the problem to incoming materials. Working closely with Finley engineers who had repeatedly tried to get the vendor to improve quality, the team finally resolved the problem by having this particular supplier disqualified and purchasing from a different one. The quality of the circuit boards improved dramatically.

Still, workers were seeing their observations and input not only be acknowledged, but actually solving some of the problems they had formerly simply had to accept. Management was recognizing their value and the employees were now truly making a difference!

TROUBLED WATERS

Not everything went smoothly, of course. As the plant manager often said, "We are now operating with an open kimono!" People were encouraged to be open, honest, and speak their minds. And speak they did. About a month after teams began meeting, internal conflicts began to surface throughout the plant. Deep-seated resentment over past transgressions virtually exploded like a volcano. There were complaints about people not pulling their share of the load in the shop and supervisors looking the other way. Some supervisors were accused of playing favorites. Many operators complained about their assigned jobs. One woman was even scorned for not taking a bath often enough!

What seemed like a constant stream of people flowed into the plant manager's office with one problem after another. Morale took a nosedive. After a couple of weeks of this steady barrage of dissatisfaction, even the plant manager confided that he was ready to stop the whole process and even talked about resigning. Still, no matter how bad things seemed, the managers held the line and continued to listen and make honest efforts to respond to every issue. Their response was absolutely critical to the program's—and the factory's—long-term success.

One example of their commitment to the process occurred when some operators accused Finley managers of choosing an individual for a promotion without following the official job posting guidelines. A meeting was scheduled the very next morning for all interested employees during which the operations director (the plant manager's boss) directly addressed the operators' concerns and resolved the issue. What was remembered long after the meeting was not the solution to the problem, but management's immediate, open, and frank response. But that wasn't the only insight gained during this period of turmoil. After a few months, complaints about the teams themselves grew louder and more persistent. Employees insisted that the way teams were structured was less than practical. Rather than resent the suggestion that they hadn't picked perfectly rational teams in their first attempt, the staff members listened. In response, the EPP staff called a meeting of the entire workforce (Note that this was possible since there were only about 120 employees. With a larger group, the core group would perform this task. See Chapter Three). They assembled in the cafeteria once again and, with the help of the staff, discussed the dynamics of good teams, the most practical number of members, and other details. Then everyone turned to a large flip chart at the front of the room. On it was a drawing of the factory itself. "Now that we've discussed this thoroughly, it's time to redraw our groups," said one of the staff members. With the lines literally redrawn in what they felt were practical ways, the employees had more reason than ever before to see this as their process.

Management also realized that the company was critically weak when it came to effective communication skills, especially in the areas of problem solving, interpersonal conflict resolution, and nondefensive confrontation. To meet the problem head-on, they conducted a four-day workshop for all employees in leadership positions. This included not just managers and supervisors, but also engineers, administrative personnel, hourly group leaders and area inspectors. The impact of this practical communication skills training was substantial and the benefits two-fold. The workshop not only provided the skills needed to effectively deal with the interpersonal issues, but served as a significant team-building exercise as well. Management, engineering, quality, and administrative support began to understand the importance of their interdependence and the value of working together. Suddenly they didn't just **have** to work together, they **wanted** to. A new team spirit began to emerge.

One of the factors hindering the effectiveness of the "new team" was that the Finley plant manager did not control the reins of the entire factory. Instead, engineering, finance, and production control personnel all reported to managers at headquarters. This often created conflict between these other groups and Finley management over work priorities, and caused confusion among everyone else over where their allegiance really belonged. The bridge team pointed out the problem to the divisional manager. Once again, the company was at a "put up or shut up" crossroads. Without hesitation, the manager went upstairs and, as a result, solid line reporting relationships were established, linking these functions to the Finley plant manager. A true "factory-within-a-factory" was established and the tide began to turn.

Then, suddenly, another obstacle emerged in a rather unusual way. No one even knew the problem existed until it surfaced about five months after teams were established. It all came about when one of the teams was invited to attend a local chapter meeting of the Association for Quality and Participation and give the management presentation for a project the team had recently completed. But to everyone's surprise, the engineer assigned to the team refused to participate. When confronted by the plant manager, the engineer pulled no punches.

"You know," he said, "during the past several months we engineers have made a lot of important technical improvements that helped reduce costs and boost output."

"Yes, that's true," said the plant manager. "And we all really appreciate it."

"Well, you say that now," said the engineer bitterly. "But all the credit seems to be going to the production teams. No one seems to notice the engineering contributions."

Even though he was a member of the factory team, the engineer felt more like a token than an equal member. Management realized its oversight and began stressing that the production teams were just one facet of the total employee involvement process in the plant. They also made certain that special efforts were recognized, whether they came from individuals, teams, or other work groups. The division between the engineers and the shop teams wasn't totally resolved until much later, but the differences were acknowledged, the engineers received the recognition they deserved, and they began to actively participate on the teams. And our friend the engineer who raised the issue? He went to the meeting, knowing his fellow workers and his superiors did indeed recognize his contributions.

LEAD, FOLLOW, OR...

One last major issue remained to be resolved, and that dealt with leadership. Despite the extensive participative process training and coaching provided to managers and team leaders, there were a few people who either would not "buy into" the new value system or could not effectively function in their newly defined roles. These people emerged fairly quickly and it soon became quite obvious to the rest of the Finley employees that this type of behavior was inconsistent with the values stated in the manifesto. Management tried several times to bring them around through additional training and coaching, but made little progress. Management had to take more extensive—and creative—action.

In one case, a supervisor who just could not perform his duties as team leader was transferred to an individual contributor job more suited to his skills. This was a "win-win" solution agreeable to both management and the supervisor himself. Once moved, the supervisor reinforced the decision by increasing productivity in his new position.

In another situation, an engineering manager covertly resisted the new Total Employee Involvement approach, especially where it meant production employees would have a voice in technical decisions that affected them. This manager eventually left the company rather than conform. As much as we would like to believe otherwise, there are some individuals who do not believe in participative management. Fortunately for the manager, there are still plenty of companies that embrace the "them and us" approach to management.

Once these issues were resolved, the stage was set and the employee involvement process began to emerge as a new way of doing business.

A WINNING TEAM

When a change takes place over a long period, it's often hard to recognize progress. Several plantwide measurement charts were developed in the first month of the Finley implementation to track changes in productivity, quality, and costs as the process evolved. The charts were also used during the supervisors' weekly standup meetings to provide feedback to the rest of the employees on how they were doing and to address immediate production concerns. As teams began resolving production problems and engineering improvements increased output capacities, gains in quality and productivity combined to significantly reduce total product cost. Employees didn't have to take anyone's word for this: They could see the good news on a steady basis.

Goals became an important catalyst in reaching higher and higher levels of output and quality. Spurred by the palatable—and measurable—taste of progress, teams devised their own charts and graphs. Many were handwritten and, as they started meeting and exceeding their goals, good things started to happen. A "Winning Team Syndrome" took hold that seemed to feed upon itself and output skyrocketed.

The most memorable example of Finley's ability to pull together in a total team effort occurred during a week when the production schedule demanded a significantly higher output than usual. Unfortunately, the company's reward system had its limits. Management couldn't offer monetary bonuses or incentive pay of any kind. Tangible rewards were limited to small tokens of recognition, but management knew it had to give employees a good reason to produce.

Up to this point, the highest weekly output ever achieved had been 3,800 panels. Finley management challenged the workforce with a new goal: If 4,800 panels were shipped, they would get an extra half-hour for lunch the following Monday. The pot was further sweetened with the promise that if 5,000 panels were produced, free coffee and doughnuts would be added, and if 5,500 panels were completed before the end of the shift on Friday, they could go home with full pay for the day. The panels had to be of first-rate quality and pass final inspection and the work had to be accomplished without overtime.

By the industrial engineer's calculations, even under ideal conditions and barring any machine breakdowns, the 5,500 goal could not be reached until after noon on Friday. Management could live with the workforce starting their weekend a few hours early—they would have earned it.

The employees first reacted to the announcement as if it were impossible, the memory of what a struggle it had been to reach 3,800 still fresh in their minds. But one operator said, "Let's go for it!" Then another, and yet another; the gauntlet had been accepted.

A five-foot thermometer chart was posted in Final Inspection with the three targets clearly marked. The "mercury" from a red felt pen began to display their progress toward achieving the goal. Just before 10 a.m. on **Thursday**, a wild cheer echoed throughout the building. The 5,500th panel had just been shipped! A red-faced but proud plant manager hastily tried to explain to the manufacturing vice president at the main plant why the employees were starting their weekend a full day and a half early. Apparently the industrial engineer had left something out of his calculations: the winning spirit of the Finley employees!

The charts that follow illustrate the results the Finley facility achieved following the implementation of the employee involvement process. The Reduction in Total Cost graph (Figure 1-1) vividly reveals the bottom line improvement in productivity. The scale is indexed to protect specific product cost information, but the more than 50 percent cost reduction per panel (generated by doubling the number of panels produced without increasing the workforce) realized more than $4 million of savings in a single year.

But that wasn't all. In addition, employees sub-

mitted suggestions that saved $50,000 in one year
while engineering documented more than $500,000
of process-related cost reductions. By June 1981, just
five months after start-up, the factory was able to
streamline to a one-shift operation with no loss of
personnel or reduction of output. (Figures 1-2, 1-3,
and 1-4)

THE KEYS TO THE CITY
Throughout the implementation of Total Employee
Involvement at the Finley facility, the EPP staff played
an active role in the process. Besides conducting
training in team problem-solving techniques and
facilitating team meetings, they served as coaches
and role models for team leaders, consultants to
management, and protectors of the integrity and principles of employee involvement. They were often
catalysts for change, encouraging managers, engineers, supervisors, and operators to try new
management techniques and allow their individual
creativity to emerge.

But as the process matured, there were fewer and
fewer instances where staff members had to step in
and clarify or resolve situations. It was clearly time
to complete the circle and let the employees take
control of the process in the spirit of true and
wholehearted employee involvement. Two Finley
managers received a week of facilitator training to
sharpen their skills in the TEI process. In November
1981, a written agreement was signed by Finley
management and the EPP staff officially turned over
the responsibility for managing the employee involvement process to Finley personnel. Now Finley
people were responsible for protecting the integrity

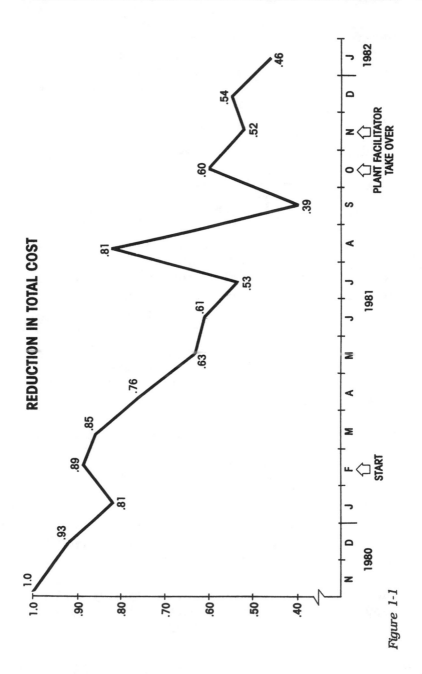

Figure 1-1

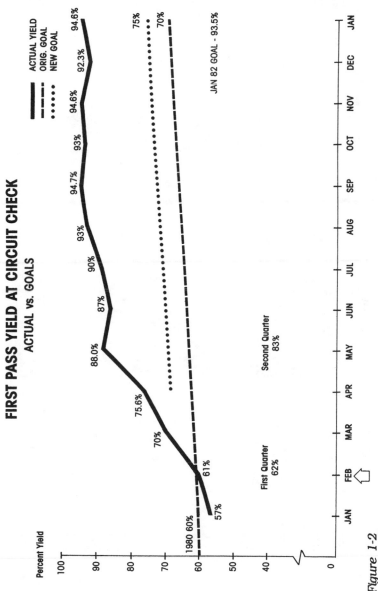

FIRST PASS YIELD AT CIRCUIT CHECK
ACTUAL vs. GOALS

Figure 1-2

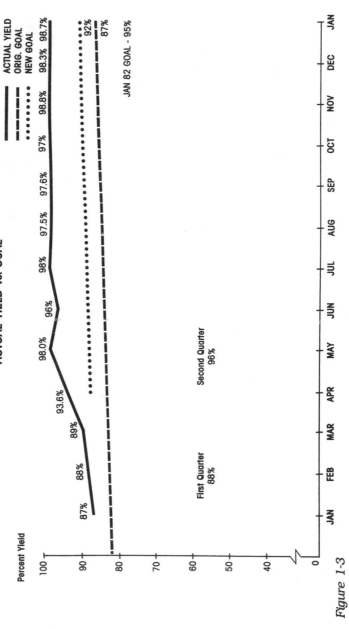

Figure 1-3

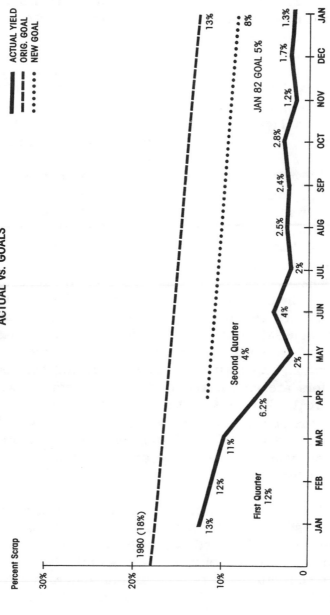

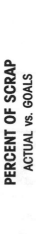

PERCENT OF SCRAP
ACTUAL vs. GOALS

Figure 1-4

of the EI process and upholding the principles outlined in the manifesto. The staff promised to conduct periodic attitude surveys like the one given to all employees at the beginning of the implementation. These would be used to monitor the progress of the various elements of the EI model (which you'll learn more about in Chapter Two) and highlight areas of concern. Figure 1-5 illustrates the trends of each element of the model measured over the first year at Finley.

Following the turnover, performance continued to increase and the high levels of quality and productivity remained steady. Finley not only earned accolades within the corporation itself, it also garnered national attention as a shining example of employee involvement success.

Back at the facility, this added an unusual and unusually pleasing reward as a means of recognition. Employees get to take part in periodic workshops conducted right in the facility for interested visitors. Guests are shown the facility by several production operators—no managers allowed. During the tour, visitors are encouraged to ask the operators what it's **really** like to work there. Afterward, the guides join the guests and members of the Finley staff for lunch and the informal, open exchange continues. Those who don't take any active part in the visit aren't forgotten, either: they get an extra half-hour for lunch!

Of all they see during their tour, visitors are often most surprised to see highly trained machine operators and skilled technicians sweeping floors, planning company picnics, reading in the team room, or discussing team projects in the hallways. When confronted, the workers quickly explain that they

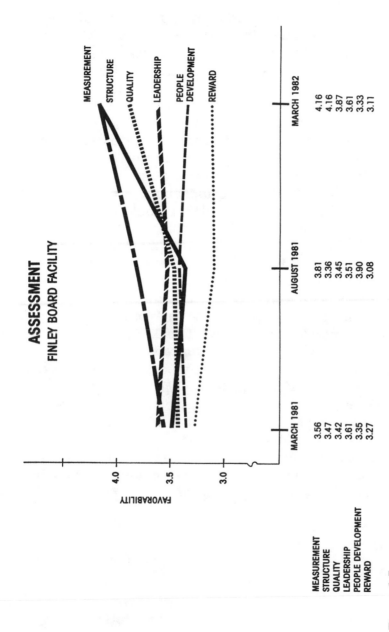

Figure 1-5

have completed their production goals or that they need to wait for another unit to complete a task before they can begin. Blasphemy? Permissiveness? Indolence? Not by a long shot. Production teams have learned precisely what is needed to produce the product in the least time, with the fewest defects, the least rework, and the lowest cost.

The employees are encouraged to be as effective as possible, and the people at Finley have finally realized that that does not necessarily mean keeping their noses to narrowly-defined grindstones. In many cases "looking busy" or working ahead would only create excess inventory and increase the risk of defective products and rework. While in most companies workers are scolded or punished if they stray from their work stations or appear to not have enough to do, this is not the case at Finley. During short periods of idle time or after achieving the day's production goal, workers are allowed to do what makes sense.

Management trusts the workers. In turn, four-hour jobs are not stretched to eight. Defects are avoided or reported and fixed. Waste is kept to an absolute minimum. And employees have the opportunity to complete team projects and make real contributions to the business.

And **the employees trust management.** There's no longer anything to prove. **Trust, quality, and true productivity are now a way of life at Finley.**

CHAPTER TWO

THE INTERNAL FRAMEWORK OF EMPLOYEE INVOLVEMENT

The employee involvement process described in this book wasn't developed from a theoretical model and then applied in a real-life work setting. The elements presented here were learned by careful examination of actual experiences, successes, and failures of efforts to increase productivity and involve people in their work in a more meaningful, fulfilling, and effective way. These findings were compared with research in organization development, social sciences, productivity improvement, and quality of worklife. As additional experience and knowledge from a variety of organizations were gained, the total scope and objectives of the employee involvement process became clearer. (For a "road map" of the process, see Appendix A.)

The elements weren't developed to intellectualize the process, either. What they do is provide a clear way to assign responsibility, to break it down into manageable chunks. In the previous chapter, we talked about one success story using the EI process. When the employees, staff, and managers were faced with a towering pile of 450 suggestions, the problems at first appeared insurmountable. But by using the following elements, the teams were able to classify the issues and thereby divide and conquer. This chapter will take a closer look at those elements that served as the framework on which they hung the process: its purpose, objectives, and methodology.

First, however, we must accept the premise that an organization can reach its maximum productivity and profit potential only if it integrates the organization's needs with the needs of its people. Typically, companies actively create structures and systems such as strategic plans, operational plans, profit objectives, production schedules, quality goals, labor accounting, and cost controls that express the needs of the organization and monitor accomplishment.

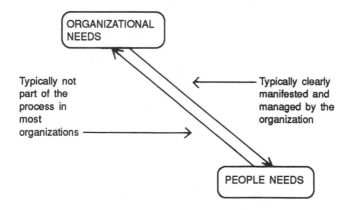

Figure 2-1

Most organizations, though, haven't bothered to create structures and mechanisms that allow people at all levels in the organization to identify, communicate, and thus fulfill their own needs so they can perform their work effectively and maintain a high quality of worklife.

One of the most often cited examples of this need for balance was the General Motors Vega plant in Lordstown, Ohio (Stinnett, 1983). The factory was to be the epitome of efficiency and productivity in modern automobile assembly, a scientifically designed and engineered masterpiece of industrial technology. Shortly after the plant began operating, workers were faced with a speed-up on the assembly line. By meeting the problem head-on, together they devised a way to work in pairs to accommodate the increased production level. But supervisors soon informed workers they weren't allowed to use a team approach. When the employees went to their managers to protest, management ignored their grievances and imposed a second speed-up. Madness!

When they failed to meet production quotas yet again, the workers went on strike. Management refused to accept the fact that they had made a mistake and quality deteriorated still further. As upper management increased pressure to conform, workers rebelled and, out of frustration, began to sabotage cars on the line. What could have been the most productive automobile plant in the country was brought to its knees simply by the organization's failure to address the needs of its people. The employee involvement process is designed to address this dimension of people needs and provide a methodology for integrating both sets of needs in order to achieve optimal organizational effectiveness.

SOUND SCIENTIFIC BASIS FOR CHANGE

As we mentioned earlier, this is no pie-in-the-sky theorizing. Much of our research is centered on the work of Rensis Likert and his many years of studying organizations and what makes them effective. In his publication *New Patterns of Management* (1976), Likert clearly outlines the foundation of successful integration of organizational and people needs and a methodology for putting the concept into practice. Essentially:

> Management will make **complete use** of the **potential** of its **human resources** only when **each person** in an organization **belongs to one or more** effective **work groups** that have solid **group loyalty**, effective **interaction skills**, and high performance **goals**.

The first statement "...complete use of the potential of its human resources..." is not just about using employees to help fix things that are wrong or solve work-related problems. Rather, the process is designed to **optimize** the capabilities and potential of every employee.

Perhaps the best way to explain this is to give an example of its antithesis. On a walk through an electronics factory, we recall encountering two women seated at a work table counting screws, putting them in stacks of eight, and neatly bundling the stacks into little packages bound with masking tape. We engaged them in conversation and discovered that they had been performing this same task for several days. In response to our questions, they told us that they had no idea why the task needed to be done or why they had been selected to do it. Further revelations were that they both were highly skilled assemblers and that one was attending college classes. This is typical of what can be found in traditional companies where the idea that an organization is like a machine is dominant.

One reason so many quality circle programs fail is that management installs them in order to provide a "quick fix" solution to productivity or quality-related problems. Circles are often viewed solely as a productivity improvement measure rather than a people development process. In other words, the organization is responding only to its own needs rather than also considering the needs of its people.

The next two highlighted parts of the statement, "...each person...belongs to one or more effective work groups...," emphasize the importance of totality in the employee involvement process. Every person in the organization must be involved and each holds membership in one or more groups. Another reason some improvement programs don't live up to their original expectations is that the team organization isn't well conceived. The teams are randomly scattered throughout an organization, have no linking structure, and membership is strictly voluntary. The result is a work unit where some people are involved but many are not, and the process achieves only a fraction of its potential capability. Some problems may be solved and some improvement may develop, but optimization is an impossibility.

As a people development process, employee involvement only works when people believe in what they are doing, which is why we've emphasized "...Group loyalty..." and "...interaction skills..." The only way an organization can function effectively is if the people that constitute it are devoted to achieving its objectives, supportive of one another, and are able to work together as a tightly knit team. Teamwork must be a part of not only each immediate work group, but also in interaction between groups in the entire organization, extending to shift-to-shift, department-to-department, and even organization to organization.

Many people believe that a **participatively**-managed organization implies a **permissively**-managed situation where there are no performance standards, employees are free to work as much or as little as they want, and there is a lack of organized effort toward business objectives. This could not be further from the truth, which is why we have highlighted the last part of the statement,"...high performance goals." High expectations, challenging goals, clear performance standards, and accountability are the keys to successful organizations and an integral part of the employee involvement process.

ELEMENTS OF EMPLOYEE INVOLVEMENT

There are certain fundamental values about the way people are treated that has an enormous impact on their motivation toward work. These values are critical to the integration of the elements of employee involvement. For people to willingly put forth their maximum effort in their jobs over an extended period of time, they must feel that they are being valued as people.

This concept is well expressed in a book (Sproul, 1981) about Wayne Alderson's experiences in a large steel mill, experiences that led him to coin the phrase "value of the person." Alderson was made general manager of a steel company that had a history of labor unrest, wildcat strikes, and major financial losses. Upon taking over the reins of the plant, he made only one significant change: he began treating every employee with love, dignity, and respect. At first he was viewed with suspicion and disbelief, but once the people learned that he was sincere, remarkable changes began to occur. The result was a highly profitable foundry with one of the best labor-management relationships in the industry. What better confirmation of treating people well could anyone ask for?

Workers cannot be threatened into higher productivity, at least not for long. Only in an atmosphere of trust and caring will people respond with positive and productive energy toward achievement of organizational goals.

Think about your own work. Does your boss (or spouse or teacher or partner) value you as a whole person, personally care about your needs, desires, and aspirations? Are you treated with the dignity and respect you feel you deserve? Are you willing to "break your pick" for this person, knowing that he or she will do the same for you?

If you are the boss, do you sincerely care for your subordinates as valuable, whole human beings, or are they just so many resources like your other capital equipment, put in place to perform some organizational function? If you're like many managers, you may be saying, "Look, I pay them good money to do their jobs. They damn well better do their work and do it well or I'll find somebody else who will. I shouldn't have to go around mollycoddling my employees when they get a paycheck at the end of the week." True, the incentive of a paycheck may get the work done, but you're fooling yourself if you think people will strive for higher productivity, better quality, greater efficiency, and reduced cost if they have no sense of being personally appreciated for their contribution.

"Okay, okay," you may be responding. "I hear what you're saying, but I have other pressures on me." Certainly this is true. Unfortunately, as pressure mounts for higher output and lower costs, the focus on getting the job done becomes so great it is easy to forget about the people being chewed up in the process. Every action taken, every decision made should take into account the impact it will have on the people concerned and whether their value as people will be threatened or enhanced.

In some countries, this need for personal confirmation is not so important. But in America, there is a certain ingrained **entrepreneurial spirit** that manifests itself through a desire to have reasonable control and influence over our jobs and the decisions that will affect our work.

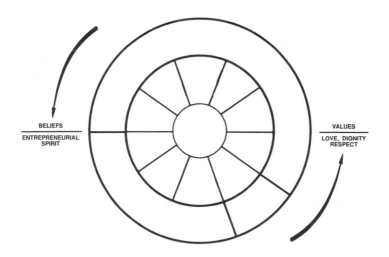

Figure 2-2

There has been a tidal wave of books, articles, studies, and reports recently about Japanese productivity, Japanese management style, and the dedicated, quality-conscious Japanese workforce. Many of these writers would have us believe we should try to emulate the Japanese if we are to compete effectively with that country in the future, but there are reasons we shouldn't or can't.

Although the Japanese have developed many excellent techniques to improve productivity and quality (most of which, by the way, they learned in the United States), there are some fundamental cultural differences that make it impossible and undesirable for U.S. businesses to become "just like the Japanese." The biggest difference relates to one of our most important strengths: our renowned entrepreneurial spirit.

Japan's culture and history emphasizes strong group loyalty, conformity to group needs, and submission to those in positions of authority. The United States, on the other hand, has a proud heritage of rugged individualism, from the colonists who came to America to escape oppression or find adventure, to the pioneers who homesteaded across the plains, to the immigrants who gave up everything in their homelands in order to chase the American dream of free enterprise. Most U.S. employees seek achievement, desire autonomy, and want to be recognized as individuals. If you question this, just look at the number of American workers who have outside businesses and hobbies. Usually this is because they are seeking the kind of satisfaction they could be but aren't getting on the job.

This is not to say that Americans are only looking out for "number one." Recent evidence suggests there is an increasing desire on the part of Americans to belong, to have a sense of community, and to make commitments to others. Companies that learn to foster this sense of community and, at the same time promote the creativity spawned by entrepreneurial spirit, will have a distinct advantage in the competitive marketplace. And this is where employee involvement comes in. EI provides a structure in which this condition may be developed so that people will be doing their most productive, fulfilling work on the job.

BASIC CONDITIONS

So where do we begin? Which of the thousands of individual issues that affect an organization's ability to optimize its productivity and provide a high quality of worklife for its employees do we tackle? Like any other situation that at first seems overwhelming, let's break these issues down and sort them into categories. The ten discussed here form a basis for defining the necessary conditions required for organizations to reach this optimal state. Six of the elements are "people" conditions, three are "technology" conditions, and the last deals with the "environment."

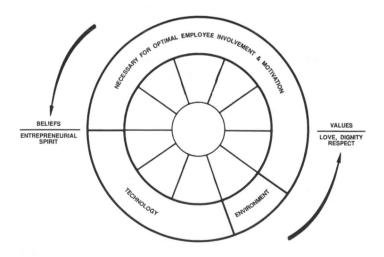

Figure 2-3

People Elements

The six "people elements" that define the conditions necessary for optimal employee involvement and motivation are leadership, structure, measurement, reward, quality, and people development. All the elements are equally important and necessary for achieving optimal effectiveness.

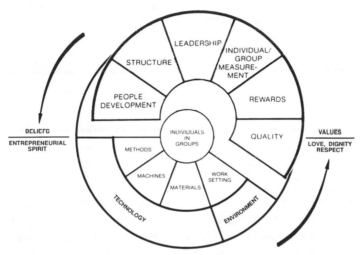

Figure 2-4

LEADERSHIP

We all know what leadership is: Theodore Roosevelt and the Rough Riders, Lech Walesa, Mahatma Gandhi, General George Custer—whoops! (But then, maybe Custer isn't such a bad example...some employees think their managers must have studied under him!) For our purposes, though, we'd like to refine the definition a bit. **As one of the people ele-**

ments, leadership is the positive behaviors of people occupying leadership roles in the work unit (managers, supervisors, engineers, technical support, group leaders) that create an atmosphere of acceptance, openness, trust, and achievement.

Like great world leaders, though, leaders in successful organizations display vision and courage by helping the work unit define and achieve its goals, allowing employees to participate in making decisions that affect their work, and encouraging each person to take greater responsibility for his or her own work. Also like their bigger-than-life counterparts, leaders in an employee involvement setting cannot abdicate their responsibility. They must remain at the forefront of the organization, setting a positive example of the behaviors desired of everyone in the work unit. To a great extent, the performance of the work unit corresponds directly to the personal performance of the leaders within the unit.

STRUCTURE

Again, let's refine this from the usual definition of "a certain pattern of organization" to mean **the pattern of communication within the work unit: who talks with whom about what for what purpose. Total Employee Involvement calls for a structure that allows every employee within the work unit an opportunity to meet in one or more groups on a regular basis to set goals, identify and resolve work-related problems, receive feedback on performance, and respond to business and personal needs.**

With long-held beliefs and experience to "unlearn," effective and meaningful employee involvement does not occur spontaneously. Management must establish well-defined structures to force the required communication to take place. The word "force" may seem a little strong, but in any change process, new behaviors such as participative decision-making will only come about if a rigorous discipline makes the desired behavior inescapable until it becomes ingrained into the normal pattern of doing business.

In a way, establishing the employee involvement structure is a little like learning to make cookies. At first, you closely follow the recipe, carefully measuring out each of the required ingredients, mixing them according to the instructions, and baking them for the specified amount of time at the appropriate temperature. Only after you have made several batches of cookies and are confident of the outcome do you begin to consider possible modifications of the recipe. The basic routine is still followed, but each variation is examined—or tasted in the case of our cookies—to assess the impact of the change.

So it is with the employee involvement process. The basic structure is followed carefully until the organization is confident in the results. Only then should modifications be made to "enhance the flavor" of the process, with each variation being assessed along the way to make sure it has the desired result. Then, and only then, should you change the recipe itself.

MEASUREMENT

For cookies, this means tablespoons and teaspoons, cups and dozens, but in employee involvement, it's **the process used to assess the effectiveness of the changes being made. There will be measurements for individual, group, and entire work unit performance, with feedback on this performance provided on a regular basis.**

People want to do a good job. There should be

little dispute of this since the overwhelming majority of American workers find it personally important to perform well on the job (remember our friends who work their fingers to the bone because they care, while no one else gives a damn?), but exactly how do you measure performance quality? Ironically, most people don't know what is expected of them on a daily basis, nor do they receive regular feedback that tells them whether they have met the expectations. Managers often wonder why people just come to work and "put in their eight hours." The answer is simple: that's probably all that is expected of them.

Although it's done every day in companies throughout the country, it is folly to expect to increase the productivity of a workforce by simply telling people to work harder. Even the platitude "work smarter, not harder," is just that, a platitude. Aside from the obvious suggestion that the worker isn't delivering ("So you're saying I'm not working hard now?"), such a directive is vague and disturbingly open-ended. If employees weren't afraid of being branded smart alecks or troublemakers, they might ask, "What do you mean, harder [or smarter]?" It's certainly a fair question, and one that deserves an answer. Unfortunately, most managers don't have an answer, because they don't know, either. (Rather than admit ignorance in front of a worker, an uncertain manager often reacts with the classic "the best defense is a good offense" approach that translates to disdain for the "smart aleck" or "troublemaker" employee.)

In a production setting, each operator should have a daily goal and know at the end of the day if it has been reached. Each work area should have daily, weekly, monthly, and annual goals, with up-to-date reports on their progress. High performance organizations have high performance goals that are clearly communicated to the entire workforce and regularly reviewed by using simple progress charts prominently displayed in the work area.

REWARD

In the Olympics, athletes receive large gold, silver, and bronze medals as concrete symbols of their achievements. **In employee involvement, rewards have their parallel in providing all members of the work unit adequate return—both tangible and psychological—for their contributions.**

Although well-designed and challenging work assignments can be intrinsically motivating, people simply won't sustain high performance effort unless they feel they are being recognized and justly compensated in return. Interestingly enough, when it comes to tangible compensation, most people seem less concerned about the **amount** of pay than about **equity**. Either employees see co-workers being paid more for work requiring what they perceive as less skill or effort, or they see someone in their same job classification goofing off all day and getting paid the same amount. **People want their co-workers and especially their managers to notice and acknowledge the extra effort they expend on getting a job done, even if it is a simple verbal expression of appreciation.**

A key factor in achieving higher and higher levels of performance is to develop a reward and recognition system that is considered adequate and equitable by all employees in the unit. Reward systems don't have to be elaborate or complex—in fact, the simpler the better. They must, however, relate directly to recent individual or group performance in order to reinforce the productive behavior and provide a sense of pride and satisfaction. For instance, in one production area the weekly quota would occasionally exceed the usual capacity of the shop. The manager would challenge the workforce to produce the required number of first quality parts without overtime by promising free coffee and doughnuts and a long lunch hour the following Monday if they filled the demand. The goals were never missed!

Of course, such a seemingly simple reward for considerable extra effort would not work in an organization that did not already have the leadership characteristics described earlier, or a measurement system that provided current feedback on progress, or a workforce that took pride in its accomplishments and knew their achievement would be sincerely appreciated.

Many companies believe that financial incentives (such as profit-sharing, gainsharing, or bonus systems) alone will be enough to improve productivity. Although these programs are good and will generate positive results for awhile, if the other elements of employee involvement described here are not also implemented, the improvement will not sustain itself and optimal results will never be realized. You can buy products, but you can't buy productivity.

QUALITY

In the consumer's perception, there's no substitute for quality. But as any producer knows, it's a long, hard path to attain it. **In employee involvement, quality is achieved with "do it right the first time" and "errors are avoidable" attitudes. Quality work means having the proper training, methods, and tools to allow 100 percent conformance to requirements every time.**

It's difficult to have pride in anything of poor quality, whether it's a product or a service, business or personal. No one is motivated toward higher productivity if he or she believes the result is substandard. Yet look at the messages conveyed every day in the workplace. Supervisors sing the slogans of quality and hang "Quality First" posters on the wall, but their behaviors send a clearer message: "We've got a schedule to meet. Get it down the line: final inspection will catch any defects," or "Ship it and let field service handle the problems." But don't blame the supervisors for this. After all, management has made it clear that if the shipment doesn't get out on time, the quarterly revenue target might be missed. It's a lot easier to hide a few customer complaints about quality than to explain to the board of directors why the first-quarter ship plan was delayed. Is it any wonder Americans are switching to Japanese products? They're simply guessing that if other U.S. companies have the same lack of commitment to quality as their own, they're not going to take any unnecessary risks.

Perhaps that is somewhat harsh. Many major U.S. corporations have finally come to the realization that consumers will no longer put up with marginal quality. The point here is that the employees who produce these products won't put up with poor quality, either. While that doesn't necessarily mean they'll quit their jobs and head for a company that puts pride in every product, it probably does mean that they won't perform the job with wholehearted dedication. **If companies expect their employees to take pride in their work and pride in their company, management must, in turn, demonstrate its commitment to providing the tools, training, and** systems necessary for producing a first-quality product or service.

PEOPLE DEVELOPMENT

A wise man once said, "The only evidence of life is growth." Employees need to keep growing personally and professionally. **In employee involvement, this is referred to as people development, which basically means opportunities for training, new learning, career advancement, and work redesign in the work unit.**

Growth in the job doesn't just mean refresher courses and moving up on the corporate ladder. Initially, it comes in the form of basic education and skill development for a current job. The next step might be to develop related skills. For instance, at Finley drill machine operators knew enough about how their machines worked to perform regular maintenance like once-a-week oiling, knowing what bolt to order and how to replace it if necessary, and recognizing symptoms of more serious problems so that maintenance specialists could be called in **before** there was a time-consuming, material wasting breakdown.

There's also cross-training, a work version of "walking a mile in another man's moccasins." It's easy to criticize co-workers when you don't really understand how they do what they do. Like the principal who spends a day on the other side of the desk, employees gain new respect for their co-workers as well as new understanding of how they can best interact with them through cross-training. Cross-training also adds flexibility, provides additional challenge, and helps employees develop a fuller understanding of the entire operation.

Finally, people can begin to examine the design of the work itself. How can it be made more personally challenging and rewarding? Can it be modified to eliminate monotonous, repetitive tasks? How can the defects and their risks be minimized?

In addition to providing continual learning experiences on the job, people must have ample opportunity to chart a long-term career growth path. This could include supervisory development, tuition refund programs at local colleges, professional society memberships, attending conferences and special workshops, and so forth.

The basic principle behind people development is sustained performance and job satisfaction, and it's dependent upon being able to answer "yes" to two questions:

- Am I learning something new on my job every day?, and
- Do I have a future in this organization?

Technology Elements

Good leadership, well-designed structures, established measurements, meaningful rewards, commitment to quality, and attention to people development are all crucial to improving productivity and quality of worklife. An organization can still fail, however, if it doesn't have sufficient technology to produce a competitive product or service. Typically, most companies devote a lot of time and attention to the "three Ms," methods, materials, and machines. There is a wealth of knowledge in technical fields such as industrial engineering, manufacturing, and process engineering, operations research, and quality control. This book can't address the entire scope of technological productivity improvement, and that isn't its point since our focus is primarily on the "people" side of the productivity puzzle. For the sake of completeness, though, it is useful to understand the technology elements used in the employee involvement process.

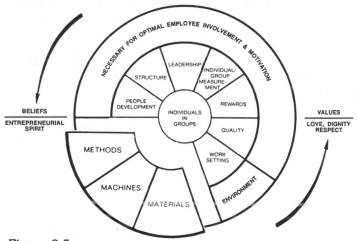

Figure 2-5

METHODS
This is the "how": the operation planning, procedures, documentation, manufacturing processes, and computer information systems that support the work being done.

The methods element is the virtually invisible skeleton on which employee involvement hangs. It includes all the systems and procedures necessary for the efficient accomplishment of work, such as clearly written and understandable operation planning that is accessible and current, a scheduling system that provides a smooth flow of work and up-to-date status of work in process, accurate and fair time standards for each operation, documentation and procedures that speed the flow of information throughout the system, and management information systems that provide the information necessary to manage the business effectively. When the methods allow work to go smoothly, employees and managers can focus on the future instead of concentrating on grasping the present.

MATERIALS

The building blocks of a project can produce a house of cards or one of granite. Obviously and concretely important, **the materials element covers all direct and indirect materials, shop and office supplies, and vendor supplied parts used in the fabrication or assembly of the product or performance of a service.**

There has been much publicity in recent years concerning the technology of materials management. The Japanese Kanban system with its just-in-time material delivery and manufacturing system has turned traditional material control practices inside out. Incoming inspection of vendor parts, expectations of anything less than 100 percent quality, and huge stockrooms full of buffer inventories are becoming obsolete in highly competitive industries. The employee involvement process dovetails neatly with such theories and can help immensely as organizations relearn materials management and convert to new, more productive systems.

MACHINES

Here's where too many companies focus the bulk of their improvement efforts. Which is not to say that **the machines, equipment, and tools used both directly and indirectly in the production of an organization's product or service** aren't important, but they are just one part of the total equation. As we've said before, it makes little sense to patch one part of a dam when the entire structure has problems.

This element includes all manufacturing process equipment, including material handling devices, storage systems, computers and terminals, work station tools and fixtures, and office equipment. In the rapidly changing world of high technology, organizations must constantly stay abreast of the latest devices available to produce high quality goods and services. Last year's technology will not compete in next year's marketplace. Successful organizations are never satisfied with the status quo, and encourage innovation and creativity. Employee involvement sharpens employees' efforts to regularly examine the technology used in their work units, recommend improvements, and implement new ideas.

Environment Elements

The last element of the employee involvement process considers the work environment itself. Although many aspects of the work setting don't directly affect people's abilities to be more productive, the environment can have a surprising effect on motivation and job satisfaction. When you think about it, that's hardly a surprise. Aren't you more attentive at a meeting when the seats are comfortable?

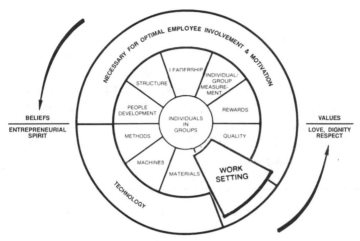

Figure 2-6

WORK SETTING

In employee involvement, **this goes beyond physical surroundings to also include employee benefits and services, company policies, and other practices related to employee work rules.**

All of these factors are included because all of them subtly affect employees' well-being. Frederick Herzberg called them hygiene factors, or "dissatisfiers." Company benefits, services, and creature comforts won't, in and of themselves, motivate people toward higher levels of productivity, but lack of attention to these factors can certainly **demotivate** employees and detract from their quality of worklife. Specifically, facility cleanliness, air temperature and quality, work station comfort and lighting, safety hazards, noise, cafeteria service, parking, recreation, health services, office and meeting room space, company benefits, and employee work rules are all factors that affect employee attitudes about their value and importance in the organization.

Interestingly enough, in organizations with traditional quality circle programs, work setting issues are generally not open for discussion, especially those related to company work rules, and employee benefits and services. At first this might seem a logical restriction. After all, these fall into the area of "management prerogative." But consider it again in terms of balance of needs. If people are dissatisfied with, say, the company policy regarding absenteeism and believe they are being treated unfairly, is it any wonder that when quality circle leaders ask for ideas to improve productivity they are met with blank stares? Ironically, the restriction on one subject directly affects another. But then, that makes sense when you realize that all of these issues are related and often entwined with one another. People are not motivated to meet company needs unless they believe that their needs will also be addressed.

During the start-up of Total Employee Involvement, groups tackle many work setting issues. This can be extremely frustrating for managers who want people to address productivity and quality-related problems. This is not subversive, however, it's normal, and people aren't asking management to give away the store. They are asking for a demonstration of good faith by management that shows a willingness to deal with employee needs. In turn, once this good faith is demonstrated, employees will direct their attention to organization needs like productivity and quality.

We have helped organizations implement Total

Employee Involvement in companies with and without unions. Successes have been achieved in both. In some union environments, work setting issues may be specifically addressed in a contract and the topic is "hands-off" for teams. We believe the contract should always be honored. We also believe, however, that the teams' ability to identify and resolve work setting issues is important to the total process. We urge the leaders of the union and the corporation to work together to find suitable mechanisms for incorporating work setting issues into the process.

AN INTERDEPENDENT SYSTEM

Any organization that truly wants to reach an optimal state of productivity and quality of worklife must direct its energy and resources into each of these ten elements. Unfortunately, there are those who would have you believe otherwise, that tackling part of the problem is plenty. Quality circle proponents think that working out technical and quality problems will get you there. Organization development consultants may say that leadership development and team building is the answer. Others suggest that "quality is free" and that focusing your effort here will garner the desired results. There are thousands of managers who are convinced that it only takes a minute! Some companies have paid these "professionals" tens or hundreds of thousands of dollars, yet wonder why things still seem a little out of sorts, or why things aren't quite as wonderful as they had hoped.

Now don't get us wrong. These management and employee participation techniques aren't necessarily "wrong." Each will likely provide some improvement.

But what they won't provide is **as much success as is possible. Optimization is achieved only through a total systems approach.** Anything less will probably mean your company will fall far short of its goal.

Individuals in Groups

One last piece of the model remains, the catalyst that links the ten model elements together. Individuals in groups is at the very heart of the diagram and rightfully so.

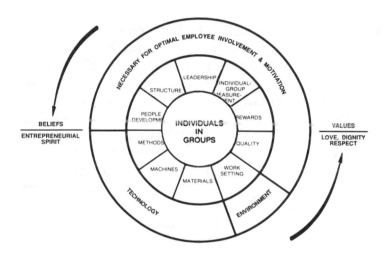

Figure 2-7

First, the concept of individuals in groups highlights the importance of the entrepreneurial spirit. Second, it acknowledges the need to reward individuals as well as groups and encourage people to use their creativity and talent to try new approaches in their work. Although their personal and professional needs and achievements certainly merit recognition, individuals are not islands isolated from the rest of the workplace and shouldn't be viewed as such. Anyone who works in an organization is automatically part of some group, whether it is a work unit, a project team, or administrative staff.

The question is not whether someone wants to be a member of a group. Rather, it becomes a matter of how best to structure and operate the various groups within an organization to achieve maximum effectiveness. The Total Employee Involvement process provides an answer to that question, and the remainder of this book describes this process in detail.

CHAPTER THREE

THE STRUCTURE
OF SUCCESS

Creating the kind of sweeping changes necessary for a truly effective employee involvement process is not easy. These changes aren't brought about simply by a strong leader, a superman who makes a motivational plea to the people who then spring into action. Rather, this transformation comes from creating the appropriate structures and applying effective group processes that allow the creativity and energy of the organization to be harnessed and focused on productive improvement.

The employee involvement process includes major structural and process actions, or interventions. Structure refers to the **patterns** of interactions within the organization, or **who** talks to **whom** about **what**. Process refers to the **nature** of the interactions. In other words, **how** people communicate with one another. Structural interventions consist primarily of designing teams and meetings of various kinds to actively begin the transformation process. An appropriate structure **allows** individuals to acquire and use new skills that will improve interaction. They will then be able to learn **how** to interact more effectively.

BASIC STRUCTURES

Two major principles drive structural design of any complete employee involvement process:

- Teams must have the appropriate membership for effective achievement of team goals and objectives

- Teams must be able to communicate easily and thoroughly throughout the entire organization.

Aside from these two requirements, the design can be fairly flexible. In working with many different corporations, we have used variations on some basic group and team structures. Some of these groups remain a permanent part of the ongoing operation, others serve a specific purpose during start-up but are otherwise temporary, and some may change in form and purpose as the process matures.

CREATING THE STRUCTURES

As you will see and as every employee must understand, everyone will be involved in the process on a regular and intensive basis. As we run through the responsibilities of each team, it will become quite obvious that most people will serve on more than one team. If your first reaction is, "So when do we get any **work** done?," it is an understandable one, and we will address it later. This intertwining of people, teams, management, tasks, and responsibilities, however, is important for the integrity of the process.

When most people think of employee involvement, they immediately think of the teams. But there are also other groups that are important in the process. We'll discuss three basic types of groups: committees, that don't deal with specific problems, but plan or review the overall policies and strategies; a group—the core group—that is essentially a congress that handles unit-wide issues with the implementation process; and the teams themselves, which work together to identify and resolve specific problems and issues.

SELECTING THE WORK UNIT

Assuming there is a general agreement between the change agent and manager about what area or work unit would be a likely candidate for a demonstration project, some people from that unit should be also included in the planning process.

As we saw in the Finley situation, the choice of the initial work unit is an important one. There are several characteristics that are important ingredients for success:

- The unit should be complete. That is, there should be identifiable boundaries and within those boundaries there should be the necessary resources for producing a product or service.

- The unit should be large enough that change will have obvious impact, but small enough to withstand many simultaneous operations changes. The optimum size is within a range of fifty to 200 employees. Such a group is large enough to make a significant impact, yet small enough to be manageable.

- The unit should be relatively autonomous. Every employee needs to be accountable within the unit so that everyone's loyalties are clear.

- The product or service should be recognizable to all members of the organization. After all, it is difficult to notice or measure change when the product or service undergoing the change isn't clearly defined and understood.

- The head of the unit, usually a plant manager or director, should have a great deal of authority and be relatively free from decision-making restrictions. Permission to experiment and to deviate from the norm is mandatory, and a "business-within-a-business" orientation is the most productive potential environment. A work unit that is held accountable for final quality and for its total cost but not restricted in its method of achieving those outcomes is also an acceptable candidate.

- Ultimately, the entire organization will have an investment in participation and will want some accountability for behaviors congruent with participation, but in the beginning, a willingness to experiment must be the rule.

- There should be some indication that the unit leaders believe change is appropriate. Enthusiasm or advocacy at this point is not a requirement, but a willingness to examine possibilities is a must.

- The personal characteristics of the unit's top authority are very important. He or she must be, at the very least, willing to spend substantial time devoted to the change project and also be willing to accept personal feedback about his or her own behavior.

The Planning Committee

Although the employee involvement process is by its very nature flexible, as in the beginning of any project the first formal intervention should always be a planning committee. For some companies, this will be the first meeting between managers and any professional change agents (who are, essentially, facilitators, trainers, or consultants) brought in from the outside.

The two-fold purpose of the planning committee is to:

- Assess, in broad terms, the needs of the work unit and to gather the resources required for employee involvement implementation, and

- Develop a sense of teamwork and an understanding of the process among its own members.

The planning committee should include all the primary decision makers in the unit with its top authority (i.e., plant manager) serving as the team leader. It is important to include representation from all support functions such as maintenance, facilities, technical support, finance, and personnel. It is also wise to include some first-level supervisors during the early stages, if not at the very start. And, of course, the change agents themselves are part of this group.

Many companies struggle over whether to hire outside consultants or to assign current employees to the project. Both approaches have advantages and disadvantages. In-house people are trusted, but often their advice is not heeded as readily as that of professionals who come in from outside. "Outsiders," however, often face a certain wariness based on an understandable caution about the unknown. Our experience indicates a need for approximately one change agent per fifty employees, during the initial demonstration project, so some companies opt for the best of both worlds and have "insiders" and "outsiders" on the team. Enough change agents (or facilitators) must be hired either on a contract or permanent basis to fully support the total process during the first year. Think of this in terms of the first year of childhood and the great importance of adequate care during that time. We will discuss this role in more detail later, but the planning committee should not continue unless this requirement is met.

The planning committee should meet at least once a week for a minimum of ninety minutes per meeting. This phase may last from three to five months.

There are several very important issues to be addressed during this time:

- What is the effectiveness of our own group? Can we become a model for other groups within the unit?

- What is our vision and what are our goals? What is it we really want for our unit and for ourselves?

- How will we get what we want? What resources do we have and what resources will we need?

- What is our organization really like? What are its strengths? Its weaknesses?

- What is our commitment to change?

Until these questions can be answered to the satisfaction of all members of the group, implementation should not proceed.

The change agent is responsible for establishing a

process that will allow the group to answer these questions honestly, openly, and thoroughly. Some of the methods used for this are discussed in later chapters. Once this is complete, the group can move on to gathering resources and learning more about the employee involvement process.

When outlined this way, the process probably sounds deceptively simple. It seems appropriate at this point to examine some of the typical problems that occur during this phase of the process. Issues that seem simple on the surface can be exceedingly troublesome. For instance, the question of team meeting rooms can sabotage the entire project if not handled properly. For every fifteen teams, there should be at least one team room that is dedicated solely for the purpose of team activities. Each room should be carpeted, equipped with comfortable furniture, white boards, screens, audiovisual equipment and ample storage for equipment, supplies, and books. The room should be approximately fifteen by twenty-five feet in size. Nothing will kill an employee involvement process any faster than inadequate or second-rate rooms.

Before you dismiss such details as hogwash, consider the message management sends with second-class accommodations. Along with the second-rate room comes the not-quite-hidden message that the process is second-rate and the excuses for canceling or not attending meetings increase at an alarming rate if there is no regular meeting place. Feeble excuses like, "I didn't know you changed rooms," or "I didn't get the memo," or "Somebody else was using the room," are employees' way of saying, "I know you don't consider this important, so I'm not going to, either. I have more important things to do than deal with second-rate projects."

STEADY AS SHE GOES

The stability of the unit's workforce is also an important consideration at this point. There are three sources of instability that can undermine the success of the employee involvement process. The first is referred to as "churn." This normally occurs in companies with narrowly-defined job classifications in the direct labor workforce. The incentive is always to strive for a different job with a higher classification. If there is little or no incentive to remain in one work unit, there can be excessive movement in and out. Employee involvement depends heavily upon the development of effective work teams, and high turnover within teams produces a great deal of anxiety, regrouping, starting over, retraining, and general disruption of group development. Approaches that provide opportunities for growth and advancement **within** the unit are far more productive, especially in the early stages.

A second source of instability is involuntary workforce reduction, better known as layoffs. Companies that balance their books by laying off people once or twice a year can never create a climate with enough trust to optimize productivity or quality of worklife through employee involvement.

Another unstable environment where employee involvement processes may not be appropriate is one where the company is in decline and employees are uncertain about the future. This topic is addressed in a study of employee involvement in declining organizations conducted by the University of Southern California (Mohrman, 1984). Based on observation of eight major companies in decline, the study's conclusion was that the conditions surrounding the decline tended to promote exactly the kind of behavior most likely to destroy an organizational change effort. Although employee involvement needn't be ruled out completely in such unstable atmospheres, establishing new programs in such situations is difficult at best.

KNOWING WHERE WE STAND

Before team meetings begin, each member of the unit should have a very clear picture of the business' needs. It is management's responsibility to be crystal clear about its production needs. The model proposed in this book encourages the use of simple performance charts and brief, regular informative meetings during which the charts are reviewed and explained. Individual and group goals should be developed and maintained by the teams themselves, but information about the unit's performance must be communicated by management in such a way that everyone clearly understands all aspects. The planning committee must insist that work unit measures are in place before team start-up.

The planning committee should also address accountability of its leaders for implementing and maintaining the employee involvement process. It is extremely unfair to expect supervisors and managers to change their behavior and become deeply involved in team activity and then ignore this aspect of their job in their development plans and performance appraisals.

Although there are many "shoulds" and "musts"

in these paragraphs, it is the underlying principles that are inviolate, not the particular solutions. A critical part of the change agents' job is to insist that the issues comply with the principles themselves, and, rather than force a favorite solution, fulfill the needs of this particular organization and its people.

The Steering Committee

This is where the truly powerful members of the organization get involved. Determining the optimum membership of this group shouldn't be taken lightly. The larger the organization, the more difficult determining members becomes, but this committee, which in essence represents the company itself, will include people such as the vice president of operations and general manager, major players who will ultimately decide if the process is a success and should be expanded throughout the company. The steering committee will address broad policy decisions concerning employee involvement, such as, "How fast do we expand? In what direction? How will EI affect the rest of the company? How do company policies affect EI? What is the role of upper management? How can they be good sponsors of change?"

Ordinarily, the steering committee is composed of the top executives at the location, his or her staff, the change agents, and any other top-level stakeholders. The group should meet regularly and more frequently at the beginning and during major expansions. More will be said about this very critical structure in a separate section, but it is important to know that nothing of any significance can happen without a functioning steering committee.

The Core Group

One of the most exciting and rewarding activities in the employee involvement process is the development and implementation of the core group. It is this group that should be primarily responsible for molding and shaping the structure of employee involvement to fit the needs of the organization. Another purpose of this group is to involve a broad segment of the work unit in planning the details of the employee involvement process and to begin developing a sense of ownership for the process during the early stages. The core group is made up of representatives from all levels and functions within the work unit. With at least one member from each level of management, each type of operation, each shift, each support function, the core group is a microcosm of the entire unit. There may be as many as sixty or seventy people in the core group. Some very important milestones in the planning process are reserved for the core group, in particular, the creation of a shared vision of the organization and a detailed proposal for the structure and membership of each team. The specific details of these activities are described in the next chapter.

Although the core group membership will likely change after teams are established and each team chooses its own representative, the initial selection of core group members must be done very carefully. The planning committee should take great pains to develop a selection process that is viewed as fair by all members of the work unit. For instance, some people become members by virtue of their role in the organization. Since there is only one plant manager or director, that level and function can be represented only by that person. If there are eleven second shift drill machine operators, however, a choice must be made and the second shift drill operators should be the ones to decide which one of them will represent all of them on the core group.

Even though the planning committee may have developed a very good selection process and clearly communicated the purpose and nature of the core group, it will nonetheless be difficult for the drill machine operators to make a choice. For one thing, they are probably unaccustomed to being asked to make decisions. Even though the planning committee has been extremely conscientious in keeping people informed about their progress, the drill machine operators may act as though they've never heard of employee involvement, a planning committee, a core group, or any of the rest of this "nonsense." Even after a careful explanation of how important the core group is and how it will help the operators get the things they need, most of them will stare with blank faces or roll their eyes in dismay as if to say, "How could you **possibly** expect me to believe this crap?" Some will slip into the "Whatever you say boss" mode. Others will whine, "Do we **have** to?" With persistence, however, core group members will get selected and for the most part, they will feel they were chosen by their peers (even if they are the only ones in the area who are willing to try it!).

This is normal. This does not mean the employee involvement process is doomed even before it begins. This is just the first, routine encounter with the usual resistance bound to be present in an autocratic organization. The problem, of course, is that people are being asked to participate in an important decision in an organization in which there is no existing structure or process for involving people in important decisions. One of the blessings in disguise here is that the people who actually end up in the core group tend to be the opinion leaders in the organization, the very people who can most influence change. As long as the people make their own choices, it's almost impossible to foul up the selection no matter how tedious or frustrating it may seem.

As a reminder, the core group should be formed only when the planning committee has finished its work and management is fully committed to implementing the process. Once the core group exists, no matter what the management says, the workforce will assume that a commitment to change exists and they will hold management accountable if no change occurs. There is an old adage that says if you agree to dance with a bear, you can't stop if you get tired and the bear wants to keep dancing. The core group signals the point of no return. Once the core group exists, anything short of total employee involvement will likely leave the organization worse off than it was before. There is nothing, after all, more dangerous than an energized, agitated, and angry bear.

The first few core group meetings have enormous impact on the organization when the implementation process truly gets under way. While the process of selecting core group members seems squishy, excruciatingly laborious, and somewhat formless, the meetings themselves can and should be executed with a great deal of precision. Careful and detailed planning is important for any meeting, but especially so for an eight-hour meeting of forty to sixty people. This, of course, becomes even more important since this is a critical step in launching the whole employee involvement process.

Now is a good time for some no-nonsense agreements about meeting attendance and participation. Every manager must make a firm commitment to attend the core group meetings and stay for the full duration of each meeting. Just as in the selection of the team meeting rooms, it's important to establish that this process is a high priority and that management is serious about employee involvement. The managers should also be carefully coached concerning their behavior during the meetings. Their full participation during all activities is required not only because their input is imperative—and it is—but because the other employees must feel like managers are partners with them in the process, not feel like a bunch of kids in a Christmas play who can hear the audience cooing, "Oh, aren't they cute!" When managers hold back, lurk in the corners, and talk to the change agents or other managers, the rest of the team members feel excluded or, even worse, spied upon. **Unless managers participate fully in all activities, people will feel either patronized or threatened.**

Some companies have tried to ease the barriers between managers and workers by eliminating external indications of their positions. Unfortunately, some such attempts may come across as artificial. For instance, when managers have been asked to dress casually for core group meetings, many showed up in brand new, carefully pressed jeans and designer label T-shirts. How embarrassingly transparent! They would have been better off wearing their normal business attire and perhaps removing their coats or loosening their ties. What you want to do is strip away pretension, so it makes no sense to ask them to pretend they are no longer the managers. Everyone knows that's baloney. Although the management role will change considerably during the process of implementation, the managers are still the leaders of the organization and it is foolish to pretend otherwise. You must keep their trust by being honest, and in this case, being honest means recognizing reality.

Part of that is making certain the managers also realize that they must be open to trying the process in order for it to succeed. Insincerity has an unmistakable and poisonous stench, one that is difficult to dispel. Managers who do not truly believe change can occur must be brought into the system through as many hours of discussion it takes, because otherwise the employees will not risk commitment to the process. No one wants to be a part of failure, and the managers must set the tone of success.

After the teams have actually been formed and had their first meetings, they'll select one of their own to represent them on the core group. The core group should meet on a continuing basis, approximately once each quarter. Its ongoing function is to monitor the progress and effectiveness of the EI process and to solve problems when they arise. Future directions of the process should always be discussed in the core group so that decisions about corrective action are shared. Once the core group is established and teams have begun operating, management should never make a unilateral decision about the process' future course.

The quarterly core group meetings needn't be daylong sessions. Experience suggests that four-hour meetings that overlap shifts are quite effective. What is important, however, is careful planning for the meetings in collaboration with a subcommittee of change agents, and core group members. The meetings should always focus on the attainment of the vision. Participants should ask, "Where do we stand? How can we move more effectively toward our vision?" Results of the periodic attitude surveys should be evaluated by the core group and checked against the perceptions of the workforce. The core group's job in this effort is to resolve any differences between the survey data and their intuitive judgments of the organization's current status in attaining the vision.

Sometimes managers have a difficult time understanding the value of the core group, because it seems so far removed from the "bottom line." But this is one structure that should not be tampered with. The change agent must insist upon maintaining the integrity of the core group. Many of the other structures—the steering committee, the teams, the bridge team—may change considerably as the implementation evolves and adapts to the needs of the organization, but the core group should hold closely to its original form and function.

The Bridge Team

Managers are employees, too. Total Employee Involvement means **all** employees share in the process of "making this a better place to work" and "becoming more productive," including managers. Yet, as we have already discussed, the manager's role is somewhat different than the line workers. The EI process recognizes this and addresses it, in part, through the bridge team. The purposes of the bridge team are to:

- Solve problems that cannot be resolved by other teams within the unit because of lack of resources or authority

- Solve problems concerning management practices or policies, and
- Address the needs of the management team.

The bridge team membership resembles the composition of the planning committee, but may be less inclusive. The top-level work unit manager is the team leader. His or her staff are members. Key support persons and change agents are also members. The bridge team serves as the primary vehicle for convincing the rest of the organization that its management team is competent and sincere about employee involvement and its goals. The credibility of the process is highly dependent upon the success of the bridge team. If this team can be counted upon to "deliver the goods," that is, to respond quickly and effectively to issues identified by the teams, the whole implementation has a high probability of success. If the team is inconsistent, slow, or weak, the other teams will tend to lapse into periods of lethargy, apathy, or hostility.

The new management function created by the bridge team implies a profound change, one that is difficult to grasp in relation to the widely-accepted definition of management's role in the organization. While management is still accountable for the unit's results and is still responsible for communicating the needs of the business, the **activities** of the organization are determined primarily by the teams. To succeed, management will have to put aside some activities it has always treated as important and focus on other activities identified by the teams that may never have been considered important before.

Managers will almost certainly feel uncomfortable with this change in responsibility. As we mentioned earlier, they will probably also feel overwhelmed and somewhat resentful of the initial added burden. They must, however, avoid the lethal trap of trying to do everything they previously did **plus** everything the teams want them to do. That is a sure formula for failure. While it's a popular fantasy that managers should consistently perform deeds of heroic proportions, this is nonsense. What the bridge team will find is that while it must take seriously every idea passed through the teams to it, this is not to say that the bridge team must accept every suggestion from the teams without question. Many of the suggestions will be unimplementable, outrageous, or trivial. Many will be test cases to see if management can be trusted. Those ideas that seem peculiar or even extraordinary must be thoroughly discussed with the teams. Each and every idea—the overwhelming majority of which will be an accurate description of what the organization needs to be doing in order to be effective—must be taken absolutely seriously and responded to with the utmost integrity 100 percent of the time. The resulting dialogue between management and employees will be so transformed when compared to previous communication, it will be almost unrecognizable. The authenticity and depth of understanding can increase far beyond the wildest expectations of anyone involved.

Much of this will not be fun and may even be painful, but the results will be rewarding. Just one example of how effective communication and trust can begin to develop is demonstrated by an incident at Finley. One team of machine operators was highly skeptical of employee involvement and hostile toward management. The members decided to prove that all of this stuff was baloney. As a team, they decided to submit an idea to the bridge team that suggested that the company build a gym and a sauna for employee recreation. "This," they thought, "will unmask these jokers." On the day they were to meet with the bridge team member handling the suggestion, the team members braced themselves for the confrontation with their best all-knowing smirks. Much to their surprise, the high-level manager representing the bridge team brought them a three-page document that outlined the estimated cost of such a facility, a fair assessment of the advantages and disadvantages of the proposal, a long list of various kinds of recreational facilities that might be far more feasible, and a discussion of similar facilities at other companies. Although the answer was no, this was hardly the flippant or harsh response the machine operators had expected. Instead, it was obvious that various managers and staff members had spent several hours investigating the proposal and preparing a thoughtful and intelligent report, **as if the idea really mattered!** When it was time to discuss the response, the team members revealed their astonishment and embarrassment. They, of course, didn't really want the company to spend a lot of money on a gym. "To tell you the truth," one of the team members said bashfully, "we thought you would just toss the suggestion into the trash can and forget it." Recognizing their own power and the opportunity to be taken seriously, that particular team started thinking more carefully about what they **really** wanted management to do.

While some people might shake their heads about "wasting" so much time assessing and responding to what might be called trivial requests, the increased trust and confidence derived from such situations far outweigh the expense. It is, in fact, priceless.

Chapter Five elaborates more on the operation of the bridge team.

Supervisor Teams

The bridge team is connected to other teams through linking members who are team leaders or members of other teams in the unit. Production or area managers will typically be team leaders of groups of first-level managers or supervisors. While they have special problems in their role as supervisors, their team functions much the same way as the production teams. They solve problems related to their own productivity and quality of worklife and identify work unit problems that need resolution by the bridge team. Unusual demands are placed upon supervisors during the implementation of employee involvement and many of their team problems focus on ways to optimize their effectiveness during the transition.

Technical Support Teams

Often, one of the most difficult challenges of implementing employee involvement is overcoming the resistance of the technical support people. "Everyone knows how independent and stubborn engineers are," is one of the comments you're likely to hear. But engineers have jobs to do and problems to solve just like everyone else in the organization. Although engineering groups or maintenance groups may require some special techniques or special designs, their teams function under the same fundamental principles as other teams.

Production Teams

These teams are composed of first-level workers. Ideally the teams are composed of six to eight (but never more than twelve) employees who perform similar tasks, and who have common objectives and a high degree of interdependency. They need each other to get the job done. The supervisor or manager is the team leader and the technical people who support the area are also members of the team. This basic structure should be non-negotiable for the first six months at least. Each team should meet for a minimum of one hour every week without fail. They should meet at the same time and in the same place every week. Team meetings should not be canceled under any circumstances. If a decision must be made between having the meeting or making the weekly schedule, **have the meeting!** There is no crisis important enough to justify canceling the meeting. (In rare instances, a meeting may be **rescheduled** to a different time that same week, but only in an emergency; e.g., a maintenance team working on a piece of equipment that has production shut down). The plant manager and everyone else in the unit can be confident that no matter how bad things are, every single person in the unit is spending at least one hour per week solving problems and thinking of ways to improve things. It can be very frustrating if you believe no one has time—or takes the time—to think about improving things. "I'm too busy to think about that" can no longer be used as an excuse. After all, what is more important than the future!

These rules, of course, apply to all the structured meetings. While this seems rigid and inflexible, changing an established pattern of activity in a unit with many years of bad habits and set ways requires drastic measures. Remember also that it took many years to establish those habits, and it will take some time to change them. That is why structure and consistency are so important in the change process. It is important that everyone in the unit learns that solving problems is everyone's business and that it's an expected part of the job assignment. The good news is that, as it becomes a part of the routine, it gets easier, And, as people get into the good habit of the structured meetings, they begin to think about change and improvement on a regular and sustained basis.

The impact of these teams has special implications for first-level managers and supervisors, and technical support people. A supervisor in a manufacturing unit could be the team leader for as many as four or even five teams plus a member of his or her own team. This means six meetings every week. Since the manager is the team leader of each team, the start of teams has a profound impact on the manager's role, especially regarding time management. If there are problems in the relationship between the supervisor and the employees, the team structure tends to force a confrontation. This is good, because it brings problems out into the open so that they can be dealt with directly.

Although it is far easier to avoid conflict than resolve it, avoiding it is unproductive. The imposition of the structure makes it very difficult to avoid dealing with problems. There are, in fact, certain highly predictable behaviors you can almost expect in team meetings if there are problems in the manager-employee relationship.

Sometimes team members or supervisors will suggest that teams meet without the supervisor. This is a sure sign of a problem. The supervisor may reason, "They will be more open if I'm not there." Nonsense! This is a devious way to avoid a confrontation. **The one cardinal rule for resolving conflict is that a problem between two people cannot be resolved unless those two people are present.** That may seem incredibly obvious, but the absurd reality is that people are very eager to talk about problem behavior to anyone but the person with whom they have the problem.

Another symptom of manager-employee problems is the deathly silent meeting. Much to the chagrin of the team leader, all the pleading for openness he or she can muster produces nothing from the team members but a few grunts, uh-huhs and "yes boss" type answers. The beauty of the enforced structure is that such a situation can only be tolerated for so long before someone finally has the courage to confront the real problem.

The membership of technical people on the production teams is often controversial for similar reasons. Engineers may see the multiple meetings as burdensome and unnecessary. The real issue, however, is often a problem in the relationship between the engineer and the team members or the team leader. Again, if the engineer is not present, the conflict can't be resolved.

LINKING THE STRUCTURES

Now that the proper people are on each team, the groups must be linked together. Each employee involvement team, whether it be a support group team or a first-level supervisor team, is linked to the bridge team via each EI team manager. The supervisor teams are linked to the operations teams by the supervisors who are the leaders of the operations teams.

The important thing is to link each involvement team vertically in the work unit so there is a communication channel—i.e., the team leader—from top to bottom. An example of one organization's structure is illustrated in Figure 3-1. Notice that the manager of Production Engineering is a member of the bridge team and the leader of the engineering team, and the manager of the first shift Shop Operations is a member of the bridge team and leader of the first shift supervisor's team. In turn, the first shift supervisors are members of their own team and the leaders of one or more shop teams. The number below the supervisor indicates how many shop teams are led by that particular supervisor. Also note that the Facilities and Human Relations managers who are members of the bridge team do not report to the plant manager, since they are not part of the work unit, but rather belong to support organizations that serve as key resources. In this example, the Maintenance and Inspection departments chose to have their supervisors become part of a total first shift supervisor's team. The "MF," or manager/facilitator, designation indicates that this person also will serve as a team facilitator, a role more fully described later in the book.

Of course each organization must tailor the structure to its own needs. Manufacturing-oriented businesses may have a similar structure to that of the example, while service-oriented companies may have a very different set-up. As long as the two principles mentioned at the beginning of the chapter are followed, you can't go too far wrong.

The whole idea is to get the right people together

EXAMPLE OF WORK UNIT STRUCTURE

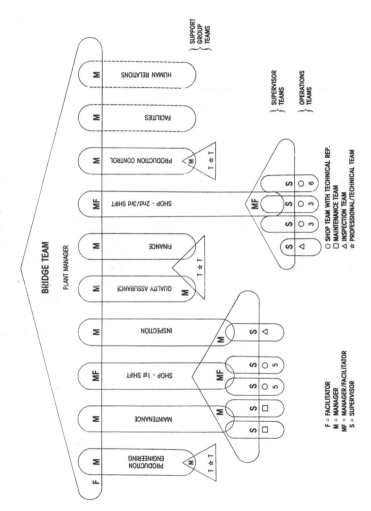

Figure 3-1

so that they can "rub shoulders" long enough to learn to work together cooperatively and productively. Without an enforced structure, those who are most uncomfortable with conflict can be astonishingly inventive and resourceful in discovering ways to avoid confrontation. Fortunately, what they will learn is that problems are less painful in the long run when they are confronted and resolved, and that many problems are merely misunderstandings. When team members begin to realize this, they will soon become eager participants and productive problem solvers. Resolving conflict becomes a positive experience and team meetings are no longer viewed with fear and trepidation.

CHAPTER FOUR

THE SUBSTANCE
OF SUCCESS

If the dark side of madness can be known by its fury and folly, then its bright side may be characterized by excitement and enthusiasm. The new experiences and learning that accompany Total Employee Involvement can, and should, be a joy. As the change occurs, different kinds of learning take place. This chapter details the nature of the change process itself and the types of learning that need to occur during each phase.

The first activity should be centered upon understanding the change process. The failure to understand the process is one of the most important reasons many training programs fail. A recent cartoon, which portrayed an indolent, unhappy-looking pig, indicates this perfectly. The caption says, "Never try to teach a pig to sing. It just wastes your time and it annoys the pig." The problem of teaching the pig to sing is, in some ways, more difficult than changing organizations. There are, however, some similarities. The pig, of course, cannot sing and could not learn to sing even if it wanted to because of physiological limitations. The problem is compounded because of the extremely remote possibility that the pig would want to sing even if it could. Unlike the poor pig, the fortunate part of organizational change endeavors is that most organizations have the capability, if not the desire, to change.

One useful change model with a long history in the behavioral sciences was introduced by Kurt Lewin (1958). There are three fundamental components: unfreezing, changing, and refreezing. Unfreezing establishes the need to change, changing—or what we'll call the transition, to avoid confusion—is the relearning and experimentation stage, and refreezing is establishing the changes as the normal way to do business. As you read the detailed descriptions of each phase, you'll begin to see more clearly why they must be done completely in the order they are presented, much as you must put one foot in front of the other to get anywhere effectively.

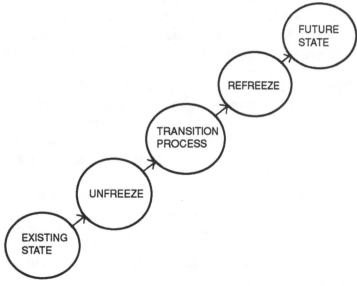

Figure 4-1

LEARNING TO LEARN

In addition, different kinds of learning experiences are required during each phase of the change process. In the unfreezing phase, the primary emphasis centers on developing an awareness and understanding of the EI process itself and establishing commitment to change. As people become more aware of what employee involvement is all about and begin to understand the need for the change along with the potential results, that commitment begins to develop. A major reason most people resist organizational change of any kind is that it alters the nature of their own role in the organization. Obviously, such a role change creates a certain amount of instability and insecurity until the implications and requirements of the new role become clearer and more acceptable. As part of the learning process during the unfreezing phase, it is essential that people understand the value to them as individuals of accepting the new role. Once they understand "what's in it for them," personal commitment to the change process is infinitely easier.

Once people have accepted the notion of the coming change and understand their roles in the process, you may proceed to the transition phase of the change model. It is during this phase that the real "skills training" takes place. Here members will acquire the necessary knowledge, skills, and ability to implement the employee involvement process. You also stand a much better chance that the training will "stick," since the people have personally committed themselves to the process and believe that the skills being taught will help them carry out their new responsibilities.

The last phase of change is refreezing into the future desired state. The learning that takes place here is designed to help people internalize the change that has occurred so that it becomes an integral part of their everyday life.

Initially, teams are an additional burden piled on top of everything else. As the teams grow and mature, the team process and the way the business operates become one and the same. When people no longer see or feel any difference, you know the refreezing phase is complete and true ownership of the process has occurred. The learning cycle is complete.

Carefully planned, well executed learning experiences provide the catalyst to put the change process into motion and aid the transition from one phase to the next. The term "learning experiences" is used here rather than the more commonly used word "training" for good reason. In a change process as fundamental and extensive as Total Employee Involvement, simple training through traditional methods of instruction is grossly inadequate. This is a base-level change in the way a business operates on a day-to-day basis and in its fundamental value system and beliefs, which in turn affect all employees within the work unit.

Changing values and beliefs is a complex and relatively slow process. It requires highly structured learning experiences that allow each individual the opportunity to examine current behavior and decide if it fits in with the organization's new direction. The experiential learning process typically follows a sequence of steps that guide participants from an existing level of awareness and understanding to a new or different state based upon the outcome of a personally felt or shared experience.

One model of learning includes five stages that a person goes through during the entire experiential learning cycle:

- Experiencing: A structured exercise (such as role playing) is conducted that allows each individual to experience firsthand how he or she feels and thinks about the particular situation.

- Sharing: Individual data generated during the experience is reported to the other participants.

- Interpreting: Individuals and the group analyze the information in relation to their specific experience.

- Generalizing: The group develops conclusions from the analysis that look at the "big picture" of the subject. Logical hypotheses are created in a more abstract sense.

- Applying: The generalizations are focused on the present environment to identify specific applications of the hypotheses both now and in the future.

Because each organization will have its own special needs and problems, the change agent or trainer must design and create appropriate learning experiences that will allow participants to develop personal awareness and understanding of the principles and a commitment to apply them in their own organizations.

The remainder of this chapter examines each phase of the change process and the specific kinds of learning experiences used with the implementation of the employee involvement process.

UNFREEZING—Awareness, Understanding, Commitment

Just as it sounds, unfreezing is a shaking-up, destabilizing, or stirring of the pot. Before change can occur, a need to change or a motive to change must be introduced and fully perceived by everyone in the system, and the organization as a whole must want to abandon its current state for a more desirable one. The activities during this stage promote awareness of the organization's shortcomings and of possible alternatives to the current state. The objective is to force the organization to examine itself and consider and assess a wide range of alternatives. The organization must, in essence, hold a mirror before itself and recognize its own true image.

Many training departments seem to have the notion that they are not responsible for creating the desire or motivation to change. It seems that training groups often work diligently to teach "state-of-the-art" supervisory or management skills that are nearly impossible for supervisors or managers to use. If no unfreezing has occurred—in other words, if people do not understand why and how they need to change—no amount of skill development will ever be enough.

Unfreezing is not about learning new skills and techniques. Unfreezing is learning and recognizing both new and old things about yourself and about the organization and is, therefore, very disruptive. Although some participants may feel exhilarated, the most common reactions during the unfreezing phase are confusion, discomfort, and fear. In a well-planned program, these consequences are temporary, but they are inevitable. If everyone seems comfortable and calm, watch out. Something's wrong.

The initial unfreezing is often somewhat spontaneous and unstructured. It is a little like the old paradox about the chicken and the egg. Did a manager somewhere in the hierarchy suddenly decide that the organization needed to change? Or did a change agent buried somewhere within the organization finally convince a key manager that employee involvement was the right direction? The answer doesn't really matter; what's important is the fact that a decision was made and the unfreezing process has begun. The task at hand is to translate the decision into action and spread the unfreezing process throughout the entire work unit.

There is a fairly careful and calculated sequence of learning experiences that must take place in order to accomplish this "thawing out" process successfully. The first step begins with management.

Management

Chances are pretty good that the top manager within the work unit has some awareness of employee involvement and agrees in principle with its implementation. Chances are equally as likely that the rest of the management team within the work unit has little awareness of what's in store for them and is too busy to be bothered by such disruptions anyway. "Employee Involvement?" they might say. "Hell, I've already got it. Last year I asked my employees what color chairs they wanted at their work stations. They voted for red, so I bought 'em red. Now, go away and let me get some work done. I'm a week behind schedule."

So initially, awareness and understanding are low. One of the first learning experiences for management is an orientation workshop. The employee involvement model and its elements are presented and fundamental values and beliefs about optimizing productivity and quality of worklife are discussed. But the most significant activity during the workshop is an exercise in which the managers examine the nature of their organization in the context of the ten EI model elements: leadership, measurement, structure, quality, reward, people development, methods, materials, machines, and work setting. Ten flip chart stands, one for each model element, are positioned around the room. In a scheduled series of timed rounds approximately one minute in length, small groups of participants brainstorm four questions relative to each element:

- What is the work unit like today?
- What would it be like if it were the best it could be?
- What are the obstacles preventing us from getting there?
- What will it take to overcome the obstacles?

At the end of each round, participants move to the next model element on their schedule, constantly intermixing the small group at any given station. This technique, called a cybernetic session, (Dixon, 1974) is a way to generate ideas in a brainstorming fashion, but with a large group.

In a very short time, a large volume of information that captures the essence of the major issues and concerns on every manager's mind is brought out into the open. The result is a sort of shared vision of the entire forthcoming change process: where the work unit is today, where it wants to go, and what needs to be done to get there. This same exercise is conducted for every group oriented to the EI process. Interestingly enough—although not really surprising—is that every group says basically the same thing, regardless of whether they are managers, engineers, supervisors, or production workers. **When you get right down to it, most people want the same things for the organization, and this exercise is the first step in developing an understanding of the shared values of the work unit.** The data from all of the groups becomes the basis for the manifesto that is developed in the core group just prior to team start-up.

Perhaps a comment about the use of the word "manifesto" is appropriate here. In the dictionary, you find the word "manifesto" defined as a dream clearly stated. We do not believe that "goals," "vision," "values," "mission," etc., capture the whole meaning or the emotional content of Total Employee Involvement nearly as well as "manifesto." Reread the manifesto developed and used at the Finley Electronics plant in Chapter One, and you can see how this document can be used as a powerful reminder of the principles that guide the process.

The second major piece of learning for managers during the unfreezing phase is an intensive period of self assessment. One approach is for each manager to take a battery of psychological assessment instruments prior to a weeklong workshop. During the workshop itself, which is conducted off-site, each manager undergoes experiences related to group development, leadership characteristics and behavior, decision-making styles, creativity, giving feedback, goal setting, and personal development. One entire day is devoted to each manager receiving personal feedback from a trained psychologist who has assessed the written instruments and performance during the group exercises, as well as from a small group of peer participants who have been observing his or her behavior during the week.

The final exercise of the workshop allows each manager to set specific personal development goals that will improve his or her performance as a manager. This workshop can be one of the key moments where real awareness of the personal value of employee involvement begins and the understanding of the manager's role in the process becomes more clear.

A third area of learning for managers consists of site visits to organizations where employee involvement is already working. This breathes life into what has been, up to this point, an intellectual head trip. It is one thing to talk about the theory of participation and what things **could** be like; it is quite another to be able to see it, talk to people involved in it, and really **feel** what it is like to work in such a company. This also gives the managers a chance to talk about their concerns with people who have been through a similar experience. When the dream can be seen as a reality, initial fears subside and commitment to at least give it a try begins to build.

The last major area of learning takes place during the planning committee sessions. As the detailed implementation plan is collaboratively developed by the management team and the change agent, a much deeper understanding of all aspects of the EI process is reached. Because every manager has a say in putting the plan together and specific responsibilities for each action are assigned, ownership and commitment to the plan and the process grow. By the time the core group meets to plan the final details of team start-up, management commitment is clearly established and this piece of the unfreezing phase is complete.

Supervisors

In manufacturing organizations, first-level supervisors are a part of management that often has some different learning requirements than those mentioned above. These people usually perceive themselves as caught between "management" and the production workforce. They must constantly walk a tightrope, balancing what seems to be impossible demands from their superiors with the needs of their subordinates, while trying to satisfy both. Supervisors typically feel overworked and underpaid, and face a great deal of responsibility with relatively little authority to back it up. And those feelings are accurate. The plight of the first-level supervisor appears to be an almost universal "trouble spot" in production environments.

Designed along the same lines as the workshop for managers, the supervisors' orientation emphasizes role definition because their role will change more than anyone else's in the employee involvement process. Most obviously, the supervisor becomes the team leader of all teams structured within his or her work group. This means that, at least initially, supervisors must still perform all their currently-assigned duties plus now conduct three to five team meetings per week. Group problem-solving skills need to be learned, team action items responded to, and team progress documented. And, by the way, it all must be done in an atmosphere of acceptance, trust, and mutual respect **while** maintaining weekly production rates.

As you might expect, this new role definition is not met with open arms. Questions—and tempers—begin to fly:

"Why should I change roles?"

"What's in it for me?"

"If I'm so important, why am I paid so little?"

"When am I going to get time to do all this?"

"Who's going to watch the floor when we're in meetings all the time?"

"Why should I treat my people with dignity and respect when my boss treats me like dirt?"

At this point in the workshop, the facilitator, who has diligently been writing these concerns on the flip chart, usually calls a break and excuses himself to the bathroom because these are tough questions, and there are no easy answers. Trying to tell the supervisors that this process is going to make their jobs easier would fall on deaf ears. Besides, it would be a lie. The fact of the matter is that starting employee involvement teams (EIT) is an additional burden placed squarely on the backs of already heavily encumbered supervisors. More than once, a frustrated voice has shouted from the back of the room, "Talk all you want about increased productivity, higher quality, less rework, reduced scrap, better communications, improved teamwork. This stuff is gonna screw me right into the ground!"

How can these issues be addressed in a positive way? Two things sometimes help reduce concern and develop a more positive outlook about the process. First, like the managers, have the supervisors visit a facility where employee involvement has been in place for at least one year. There they will get a chance to see the operation in action and, more importantly, talk with fellow supervisors who have been through the hell they are imagining is now in store for them. What the visiting supervisors discover is usually this: Yes, it is hell for a time, extremely demanding and frustrating. After awhile though, as all employees begin to understand and perform in

their new roles, the burden lightens. Many responsibilities that were once the supervisor's are now accomplished by subordinates. Less time is required
to monitor the employees and give work direction
because expectations are more clear and are "owned"
by the employees. The problem-solving process has
eliminated many of the daily production hassles that
used to gobble up the supervisor's valuable time.

The second way to address the supervisors' concerns during the orientation is to clearly acknowledge the validity of their fears and make a contract
to address specific issues as they arise. A large
block of time is set aside during the workshop to
identify issues related to implementing employee involvement. The supervisors are then asked what
would have to happen in order to eliminate the
potential problems. Usually the major concerns are
related to management commitment and support.
Management and supervisors need to discuss openly and frankly that productivity may slip during
initial start-up, that the supervisors can't be in
their areas as much, and that responding to team
issues in a timely manner is a priority. **Once the
supervisors believe management sincerely wants
the process to work and will help them through
the rough times, then they become much more
willing to make an honest attempt.**

Technical Support Teams

The third key group of people critical to the success of EITs are the technical support organizations.
Each production team has a crucial member, the
appropriate engineer or technical person that sup-
ports the production process in that area. In most

manufacturing settings, this is a new and often un-
welcome role for the engineer. Like the supervisors,
the already overworked engineers see the estab-
lishment of teams as just another burden.

During the unfreezing phase, a special
workshop is conducted with the technical support
personnel to clarify and discuss the ramifications
of their altered role. The workshop is similar to
that for the supervisors, only with the emphasis
now placed on the role of the engineer and the
issues and concerns that will arise for him or
her.

As with managers and supervisors, the engineers'
participation in the EIT process is not voluntary.
In the early stages of implementation, this normally
causes considerable hostility and resentment. They
do not readily accept having to spend an hour or
more a week in production team meetings, but
probably of even greater concern is the additional
burden of having to address technical problems
identified by the teams that fall within their responsibility. Like the supervisors, the thrust of the orientation workshop is to address these concerns, allow
them to interact with fellow engineers who have
been through the process before, and gain commitment from management to support them in the
process as it unfolds.

Besides serving as technical members of production teams, the engineers also form their own technical support team, led by their manager. During
their orientation, they begin to think about the
kinds of problems they would like this team to address. This helps the engineers understand that
employee involvement is meant to meet their needs
as well as those of the production teams.

Production Employees

Unfreezing for production employees takes place first through core group activities. There are a few large group meetings with all employees to communicate the status of employee involvement planning activities, but these are largely information sharing and awareness sessions, not learning experiences. The real learning and understanding begins in the core group.

As you recall from Chapter Three, the core group is a diagonal slice of the total work unit, composed of managers, supervisors, technical support personnel, and production operators from all work areas and shifts. The operators from each shop area meet in advance to select people who will represent them at the core group meetings.

During the planning phase of the implementation process, the core group meets twice, each time for one full day. The initial meeting is focused on two primary activities. The first is a detailed explanation of the purpose and process of employee involvement. The intent is to arm the core group members with as much information as possible so that they can, in turn, share the information with their work groups back in the shop. This is the first small step in getting members of the work unit at all levels, but particularly production operators, to begin feeling some ownership of the EI process and responsibility for supporting it in the work area.

The second major activity that day is an elaborate cybernetic session similar to the ones used earlier in the management and supervisory orientation workshops. As before, the brainstorming focuses on what the ideal work unit would be like with respect to the ten elements of the EI model (leadership, structure, etc.). All of the data is recorded and then shared in the total group. This is a key event in the un-freezing process because, as the data is reviewed, the core group members begin to realize how managers, supervisors, operators, and technical sup-port all have similar desires. A new understanding dawns as they realize that they all basically want the same things: a productive, profitable, vibrant company where people like to work. This realization is often a major learning experience for the members of the core group. The confusion and conflict seems to arise out of how they go about achieving these goals.

During the two-week interlude between the first and second core group meetings, small teams of core group members take the cybernetic session data for each model element and distill it to capture the es-sence of the information. The product from each group is a one or two sentence statement for each model element of what the ideal work unit would be like for their particular organization. At the second core group meeting these statements are combined into a single document, reviewed, refined, and finally agreed upon by the total group. As we discussed in the management unfreezing section, this document then becomes the manifesto for the work unit, the dream of what things could be like, the vision to work toward in the future. This activity is a powerful learning experience for the members of the core group. When the plant manager stands before them at the end of the day and reads aloud the manifesto they have developed together, there is a strong sense of ownership at all levels of the organization, and a feeling of responsibility to begin living up to the intent of the document.

The other major objective of the second core group meeting is to actually identify and structure the unit's employee involvement teams. Members are given some basic criteria about group composition (e.g., interdependence of members, size limitations, and the like) and then turned loose to establish their teams. Again, the collaboration and participation by all groups at all levels increases the sense of ownership and willingness to participate. Following this meeting, the manifesto and proposed team structure are shared with the rest of the organization for review, modification, and approval. This essentially completes the unfreezing phase of the implementation process. The bear is ready to dance and the orchestra is about to begin.

TRANSITION

The changing, or transition, phase involves acquiring new skills, experimenting with new behaviors, experiencing new models, and beginning to sense the new shape. Alternatives are made clearer and directions seem more tangible. Many organizations already have large training departments, facilities, and programs appropriate for the transition phase in place and can't wait to dig in. A common mistake of most "would be" change projects, in fact, is trying to jump into transition activities before unfreezing has occurred. Obviously, this type of activity is more concrete and gives the appearance of making greater strides. But the false feeling of accomplishment doesn't last long, for those promoting the change soon experience what appears to be resistance and then attack management for being insincere. What has actually happened is that they've skipped the unfreezing step. Extensive training departments, skilled instructors, libraries, and audiovisual capabilities can be wonderfully helpful during transition, but are almost useless before it.

Skill Development

During the unfreezing phase of the change process, organizational members acquire an understanding of the upcoming change, determine how they will fit into the process, and develop commitment to support the process. The next step is to acquire the necessary tools, knowledge, skills, and abilities in order to effectively **perform** in the new roles. Here is where the "training" occurs, and again, it takes place in a relatively ordered sequence of steps.

TEAM LEADER TRAINING

Several weeks in advance of starting the actual EIT meetings, a team leader training workshop is held to teach the skills necessary for leaders to conduct effective team meetings. The workshop has three major components:

- Group problem solving
- Group communications
- Group process

Group problem solving primarily covers the techniques commonly associated with quality circles. The training is divided into individual modules that cover such topics as goal setting, problem identification, prioritization, data gathering, cause and effect analysis, generating and analyzing solutions, and management presentations. A behavior modeling approach is used to acquire the individual skills associated with each problem-solving step. In it, participants first learn about the particular technique via written or video instructional material. They then view the technique being used in a mock team setting by a skilled leader. Finally, each participant has an opportunity to practice the skill in a controlled setting and receive feedback about his or her performance.

The group communication section of the workshop looks at several principles of effective communication, but focuses on listening skills. We have found that in the early stages of employee involvement team development, the most important ingredient team leaders need is good listening skills. Actively listening to the problems and issues identified in the first few meetings builds trust between the team leader and team members and encourages people to open up and say what is really on their minds. A more extensive communication skills workshop is conducted later for all work unit leadership. This will be discussed in the next section.

The third component of team leader training deals with group process. The term "group process" is often bandied about and probably has a different meaning to each person who uses it. We are referring to the three basic elements associated with the function of every team in a problem-solving situation:

- Purpose
- Content
- Process

Purpose answers the question **"Why** is the team getting together?" With employee involvement, the purpose is to improve productivity and to enhance quality of worklife. Content addresses the question **"What** is the team going to work on?" The answer might be to examine the excessive scrap rate of a particular part and find ways to eliminate the causes. Finally, there is process, which answers the question "**How** is the team going to function in order to solve the problem?"

Some factors associated with group process include how the team makes decisions (consensus, majority vote, team leader decision, etc.), the level of participation by team members, and the norms or "code of conduct" the team establishes (openness, trust, start on time, etc.). During the workshop, future team leaders learn group process and techniques that maintain team members' involvement and self-esteem, promote participation and creativity, and build trust and credibility between the team leader and team members.

The week prior to team start-up, new team leaders are again brought together for a short refresher and to prepare them for the first few meetings. It is here that an internal consultant can be invaluable to assist the team leaders in developing detailed agendas and coaching them on how to be most effective in the early phase of team development. Each event can be planned and reactions anticipated so that the team leader becomes more confident in his or her new role. We have found that the more comfortable and self assured the team leader is in the first meeting, the more open, willing, and at ease the team members become. This type of coaching by the consultant or facilitator continues on a regular basis until team leaders mature in their role. This will be discussed in more detail during the refreezing section.

TEAM MEMBER TRAINING

The training of team members takes place primarily within the weekly team meetings themselves and focuses on three elements:

- The employee involvement process
- Problem solving
- Group process

During the first couple of meetings, the teams are given a more detailed explanation of the employee involvement process, its purpose and objectives, and the workings of the teams. The organization's manifesto, which had been developed by the core group, is reviewed and discussed in light of team process goals. The team members also get to know one another on a closer, more personal basis through a paired interview technique or some other means of personal sharing. The purpose of these initial sessions is to begin focusing members' attention on their identity as a group and to develop a common understanding of the purpose for their team.

The problem-solving skills training is essentially the same as that presented in the team leader workshop, but the techniques are now taught by the team leaders. The skills are also presented on a learn-as-you-go basis rather than in their entirety up front. Following a brief overview of the entire problem-solving process, the team learns and then engages in the first problem-solving step before learning another skill. For example, the first step in the process is to identify problems and issues through brainstorming. The purpose and guidelines for brainstorming are presented and the team immediately begins using the technique to list their issues.

Only after completing this step is the team instructed in the next step: prioritizing the items on their list. This training methodology is used for two reasons. First, the team can get involved in real problem-solving right away, rather than going through several weeks of skill training. Second, if a skill is taught several weeks in advance of when it is needed, it is usually forgotten and has to be reviewed and taught again later. Thus the teams are in a constant state of learning for several weeks as they acquire and apply new skills to their team problem. This phase of the learning process is not complete until after the team has given its first management presentation. The team is then ready to try a new problem on its own.

Group process is also emphasized as an important part of team member training. Norms of behavior in the form of a team code of conduct (Figure 4-2) are identified and agreed upon. The importance of openness, honesty, and individual responsibility are discussed as essential ingredients of team success. As in team leader training, team members learn that group process—the "how" of the problem-solving process—is equally as important as the "what" and the "why." The team facilitator primarily assists the team in developing effective group process techniques. A few minutes are set aside at the end of every meeting to quickly go around the group and allow each team member to express how he or she thought the meeting went. Some questions to raise are

- Was it productive?
- Did it flow smoothly?
- Was the agenda followed?
- Did everyone participate?
- Was progress made on the team problem?
- Was consensus reached on the decisions?

This weekly assessment helps the team focus on its own performance process and effectiveness. When things go wrong, the team has an opportunity to dis-

TEAM CODE OF CONDUCT

1. Create an atmosphere of honesty, caring,
   and trust.

2. Respect every member of the group.
   —Please don't interrupt when someone
     is speaking.
   —Listen attentively.
   —Give everyone a chance to participate.

3. Be open-minded during discussions.
   Remember, no one is right all of
   the time.

4. Participate. Don't just sit and gripe.
   Problem solving is everybody's business.

5. Help make each TEAM a harmonious
   group working to improve work
   conditions and increase productivity.

6. Enjoy TEAM.

Figure 4-2

cuss what happened and how to avoid future oc-
currences. When things go right, the "go-around"
allows the team to celebrate its success and reinforce those behaviors that enhance its effectiveness. We cannot overemphasize the importance
of training teams in group process and paying
continued attention to it on a regular basis. Let's
face it, the whole point of employee involvement
is one large group process! If the employees can't
achieve success in a small group, it's unlikely
that the organization as a whole will be successful, either.

COMMUNICATION SKILLS WORKSHOP FOR ALL LEADERS

One of the most important parts of employee involvement training is a communication skills
workshop conducted for all leaders in the work unit.
In this context, "leaders" does not just refer to
managers and supervisors, but also includes
everyone in the work unit who must influence
others to get their job done. That means engineers,
production control personnel, group leaders, inspectors, technicians, dispatchers, floor planners,
and other indirect employees. Effective communication skills are as important as technical expertise
to optimize the relationship between production
operators and the various support groups. Most
conflict that arises between these groups is not due
to technical problems, but the inability to effectively
communicate with one another in a constructive
manner.

The communication skills workshop is an intensive,
thirty-two hour, experientially-based training program. Although many areas of interpersonal and
group communication are covered, the workshop

focuses on four primary skills:

- Active listening
- Nondestructive confrontation
- Interpersonal problem solving
- Conflict resolution

Much time is spent practicing the specific behaviors and skills associated with effective communication in each of the above situations. The course is long on practice and short on lecture, since the point is to help participants interact more effectively rather than learn a lot of theory about communication.

A note should be made about the timing of the workshop. It may be most effective to conduct this course after the EI teams have been meeting for six to eight weeks. At this point, organizational leaders have been involved in the process long enough to begin realizing that they need to improve their ability to communicate with others in the work setting. Conflicts are becoming more evident and team meetings often break down due to misunderstanding, lack of agreement on issues, and inability to reach consensus on decisions. Team leaders and members become increasingly frustrated with these communication breakdowns and are "ripe" for something that will improve the situation. The four-day workshop provides the answers and skills they now need. Dramatic changes in the leaders' effectiveness are often seen in the team process immediately following the workshop, and these are sustained and improved in the weeks that follow.

FACILITATOR TRAINING

The team facilitator plays a key role during all phases of the change process. Initially, this role may be filled by a professional change agent, who provides full-time facilitation services while teams are being formed and during the early stages of team development. It may also be possible prior to team start-up to train a select group of key people from within the organization to fulfill this responsibility. In either case, it is essential that the client organization learns to facilitate the employee involvement process after the initial implementation. The role of team facilitator includes assisting the team leaders in training the teams in group problem-solving and group process, coaching team leaders in improving effectiveness with the group, interfacing with management to resolve EI process-related issues, and helping protect the integrity of the employee involvement process as outlined in the organization's manifesto.

As the employee involvement process evolves within an organization, the role of management begins to change from the traditional decision-making, authoritative model, to a more facilitative one. For this reason, either managers or senior-level individual contributors who have a high degree of credibility within the organization are probably the best candidates as "internal facilitators." The primary objective is to develop a deeper sense of ownership of the process by those people in leadership positions within the organization. One way to cement this commitment is by having them become the primary facilitators of the process as part of their everyday responsibilities.

The training for this role has several components:
- Problem-solving skills
- Communication skills
- Group dynamics and group process
- Co-facilitation

Problem-solving skills are important because the facilitator needs to have equal or greater knowledge than the team leader about the problem-solving process and the various associated techniques in order to become an effective coach and trainer.

Facilitator training builds upon the communication workshop discussed earlier to include specific situations where the skills of active listening, confrontation, and conflict resolution can be best applied in the team setting.

Group dynamics and group process are the primary emphasis of the facilitator training workshop. Substantial time is spent learning process observation techniques, developing effective intervention skills, understanding the concepts of group development, and practicing how to coach and give feedback to teams and team leaders.

Finally, following the facilitator training workshop, the internal facilitators are paired with professional facilitators and together attend actual team meetings for approximately six weeks. During this time, the "trainees" become the team facilitators, making interventions, and coaching the team leader as they deem appropriate. The professional facilitators give the trainees feedback and coach them on improving their observation and intervention skills.

Like the learning experiences discussed earlier, facilitator training is very experiential in nature, focusing on skill development and practice more so than theory and concepts. Theory is an important part of the learning process, but in order for the theory to take hold and become effective, it must be learned in a setting where the participants are able to apply the skills, receive feedback, and develop applications that have meaning for them.

REFREEZING—Internalizing the EI Process

Refreezing is simply making the changes a part of the normal way. The new approaches and behaviors become more comfortable and sensible. One interesting result of this comfort is an earlier-than-expected assertion from employees that "We've always done it this way," even if they were there before the change began. But that isn't hard to understand when you realize just how strong the sense of ownership is. Success and responsibility is a very heady brew. Although the awareness of the internalization may be somewhat higher in training departments than their recognition of the need for unfreezing, these departments often fail to plan for this stage of change. "We taught them the skills, but they won't use them," is often the cry. Now is the time when employees are ready and willing to take greater control.

Refreezing is one area where the structures we discussed in Chapter Three become extremely important. A common weakness in most organizations is the inability to design structures that will support the new skills and allow the organization to successfully move into the third phase, refreezing. If the supporting structure is missing, all of the new skills, all of the hard-earned progress made up to the point of refreezing, can fall to the floor in a useless jumble. Again, it becomes more obvious why the process must be executed completely and in order.

In the case of employee involvement, the time for refreezing arrives as team meetings begin to feel like a normal part of the work routine rather than an additional burden to be borne by supervisors, managers, and employees. There are learning experiences that help people develop a sense of ownership and process permanency during this phase. One extremely effective experience is allowing members of the organization to talk to visitors about employee involvement. This includes having production operators conduct tours through their areas, permitting the guests to ask questions about the team process, the work environment, and the area in general. Work unit leaders are encouraged to visit other organizations, both within and outside of the company, to explain the employee involvement process and the way it works in their particular unit.

Members of the work unit also are responsible for conducting orientation sessions for new employees who are entering the employee involvement process for the first time. Team philosophy and process are discussed along with the manifesto. This continual process of verbal affirmation firmly implants the notion of employee involvement as an integral part of the organization.

Another activity that helps integrate the EI process into the normal routine is conducting a meeting of the core group on at least a quarterly basis to examine the effectiveness of employee involvement since the last meeting and recommend ideas for improvement. This demonstrates a clear commitment to the future success of the process.

A NEW PRESENT STATE?

The change process is not a static, linear sequence of events, but rather a dynamic, cyclical process in a constant state of evolution. No sooner does an organization reach a point of refreezing a new change, than this once-desired state becomes the new present state and the change process is ready to begin anew.

"What?" an employee might ask. "You mean I've worked my tail off for a year to get to this point and now I have to start all over again?" No, they can be assured, that's not it at all. The organization and its people have reached major milestones in transforming the company into a more productive, participative work unit. There may now be other interventions, however, that will bring even greater improvements and increased employee satisfaction. Ever-changing business, political, and social environments dictate that organizations continually examine themselves and modify their visions to remain healthy and successful. Once implemented, employee involvement allows organizations to quickly and effectively respond to changes in the world around them.

Some specific ideas for further enhancement of the employee involvement process will be discussed in the final chapter. **New learning is a key ingredient to the continued success of the process.** Training and education is not a single incident. People need constant challenge, new goals, new experiences, and new ideas. New learning experiences need to be an integral part of the initial change process and the ongoing development of any organization.

CHAPTER FIVE

THE PROCESS OF SUCCESS

No one knows the problems of an organization better than the people who live with them every day. That's why the teams, which are set up throughout the work unit, are an integral part of the employee involvement structure. The teams' primary purpose is to identify and resolve the problems that are preventing the organization from achieving its goals and its vision. These may be technical problems that affect productivity, or they may relate to quality of worklife issues that affect satisfaction with the overall working environment. A team process is required to effectively tackle such problems and issues.

As we have already mentioned, when a team is initially formed, one of its first activities is to identify those things that are preventing the group from reaching its ideal state. Typically, each team will list from forty to 100 separate items in its first brainstorming session.

Two clear distinctions between the Total Employee Involvement process and a traditional quality circle process are noteworthy at this point. First, in the issue identification phase, quality circles normally limit the team to technical issues affecting productivity and quality. As we have discussed, in the employee involvement process teams are encouraged to also include issues relating to leadership, reward and recognition, policies and practices, performance measurement, work rules, advancement and personal development.

Second, once the problems are identified and priorities established, the quality circle selects one problem to solve while the remaining thirty, forty, fifty or more issues go unattended. This can be extremely frustrating for the members of the quality circle, as each problem may take weeks or months to resolve. People expect the circle will solve all these problems, but the team quickly realizes that working through the entire list is going to take a long, long time. These two problems—failure to address worklife issues and inability to resolve problems quickly—has caused the downfall of many a quality circle program.

Figure 5-1 illustrates a process to deal effectively with both of these circumstances. Following the initial brainstorming session, the team examines the list carefully and categorizes each item in several ways. First, the team assigns a priority to every item based upon a set of criteria determined by the team, such as potential savings, time to resolve, resources required, interest to the team, and so forth. The team then looks at the top priority items and decides if they are potential team problems or action item issues.

A team problem is one that:

- Will require more extensive analysis
- Does not have an obvious solution, or
- Needs a total team effort to resolve.

It also falls within the team's realm of responsibility. The team is able to implement the solution on its own or make specific recommendations for the

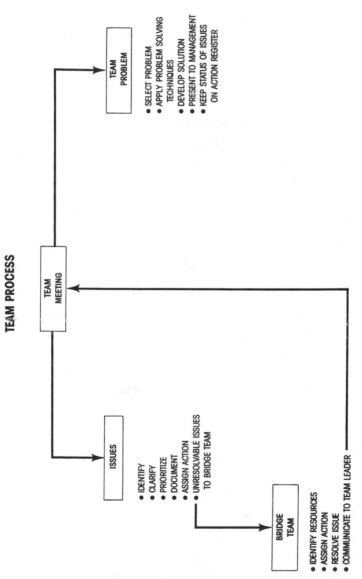

Figure 5-1

bridge team's approval.

Action item issues:

- Have a clear solution and can be resolved by one or more team members, usually outside the team meeting (e.g., write a work order to replace a leaking valve), or

- Are beyond the limits of the team's authority or area of responsibility (For example, the management practice of tracking personal absenteeism and how it is used in annual performance appraisals).

Each of these possible circumstances demands a process that the team can use to reach final resolution.

TEAM PROBLEM

An item identified as a team problem is addressed using the same sort of processes and problem-solving techniques as quality circles. Figure 5-2 shows the sequence of steps a team employs to complete the entire problem-solving cycle. Because there are innumerable materials, books, slides, videotapes, and such, that outline this kind of problem-solving process in detail, we won't go into it here. As we've said before, however, what is important is establishing a process and sticking with it.

ACTION ISSUES

Most issues identified during the brainstorming process fall into the category on the left side of Figure 5-1. The way these issues are managed is a critical ingredient in the ultimate success or failure of the employee involvement process. The key, particularly

PROBLEM SOLVING PROCESS

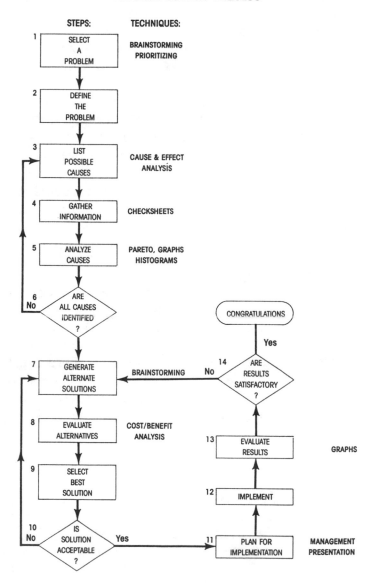

Figure 5-2

in the early stages of implementation, is quick, meaningful response to the issues. Here's how it works.

As the team clarifies each issue, it is documented with a concise problem statement and assigned a priority. An A, B, C priority scheme works well for this, with an A being a high priority issue that needs immediate attention, a B one that is important but not of immediate concern, and a C a less important issue that can wait until the others are addressed. The team then determines who will be responsible for handling each issue. As mentioned previously, the items fall into two categories: those the team can resolve and those that are beyond the team's authority. Most of the issues fall into the former category, since the area supervisor and the appropriate technical support person are members of the team. Many of the technical issues fall within their normal areas of responsibility and they can take immediate action to resolve the problems without any additional help.

When practical, one of the other team members will volunteer to assist with the issue. This serves two purposes. First, since the supervisor and engineer are normally already overloaded with work, the other team members can help by serving as additional arms and legs to gather information, make calls, write work orders, etc. Second, the team members begin learning to take on additional responsibility, develop relationships with support groups, and gain an appreciation for what it is like to work an issue through the "system." This is especially valuable for production employees. Often an impatient employee who constantly complains about how long it takes to see action becomes more tolerant when he or she is involved in the details of the process.

Eventually, team members will begin volunteering for action items on their own after developing confidence in their abilities and knowledge of the process. Teams can track the progress of each issue with a Team Action Register, such as the one illustrated in Figure 5-3, until it is resolved.

The other category of issues, those that require resolution at a higher level of authority, are sent to the bridge team. Often these issues concern management practices, plantwide or unitwide problems, or personnel policies. With these action issues, the team develops a clear statement of the problem and documents it on the Bridge Team Problem Register, Figure 5-4.

At the regular bridge team meeting, new issues are assigned action responsibility. One effective method is to have each bridge team member take responsibility for one of the model element categories: leadership, measurement, structure, people development, methods, machines, materials, work setting, quality, reward. This does not mean the person has to resolve every issue assigned to his or her category, but it does mean that the member is responsible for managing those issues. This would include assuring that an appropriate person investigates each problem, reporting status of the issues, and communicating each response to the originating team.

There are three possible responses for each issue sent to the bridge team. The first is that the problem is resolved and the solution is communicated back to the initiating team. The second possibility is that the problem is recognized as a legitimate need, but something is preventing its immediate resolution. For example, current budgetary constraints or resource limitations may not allow the solution to be imple-

TEAM ACTION REGISTER

Team: _____ Sheet _____ of _____

ITEM	DATE M/Y/D	PROBLEM DESCRIPTION	WHO	WHEN	STATUS/ COMMENTS

Figure 5-3

PROBLEM REGISTER

TEAM NAME:_____DATE:_____

ISSUE NO.	ORIG. DATE M/D/Y	ACTUAL SOLVE DATE	PROBLEM DEFINITION	CATEGORY	ISSUE PRIORITY A	B	C	RESPONSIBLE PERSON / WHEN?

Figure 5-4

mented until some time in the future. In this case, the team is presented with the information and given a plan, an estimated timetable for resolution, and the name of the responsible manager. The third situation is one where the decision is made to not resolve the issue. Especially in this case, the initiating team must receive a clear explanation of why the decision was made and how the conclusion was reached. Each "no" response should be communicated in a face-to-face meeting with ample time for questions and discussion.

In all three cases, the final ownership of the solution and satisfactory resolution of the issue resides with the originating team. If the team is not satisfied with the proposed solution or does not accept the explanation for the delay or inaction, it may choose to keep the issue open. Further investigation or negotiation may be necessary until both sides clearly understand all aspects of the issue and can reach an agreement on the best course of action. **The key principle here is that no issue is closed until the originating team agrees to close it.** In rare cases an impasse is reached, but both parties know what the differences are and accept responsibility for the consequences.

This process has many additional benefits besides simply getting problems resolved:

- The structured approach and documentation assures that once an issue is identified, it doesn't get lost or ignored. Specific responsibilities and due dates are assigned and the registers are reviewed and updated regularly. Stalled projects are highlighted so decisions can be made about what needs to be done to get them moving again.

- The required communication steps assure that each issue is clearly understood from all angles and the reasons for each decision are discussed with the originators.

- The process fosters the development of a closer relationship and better two-way communication between the teams and the work unit management.

- Through the open, honest, and frank discussions that take place in the resolution of the issues, credibility and trust can develop at all levels.

Of all the many dimensions of employee involvement, the business of management credibility is by far the most important and is also the most difficult to achieve. There are two points in the overall implementation process where the probability of failure is the highest. Both are management credibility issues. The first is the point at which employees are asked to identify issues. If management attempts to restrict the input, its credibility is lost and the process will never get off the ground. Workers will perceive the process as "one more corporate initiative," and retreat into a collusion of silence with their managers. "What lovely new clothes the employer is wearing," they'll whisper to each other with knowing smiles.

The second point occurs after the issues have been identified and employees are waiting to see what happens. Management will be tested, sometimes unfairly. Nevertheless, they must pass the test. To pass, managers must assume the burden of proof. That is, rather than communicating to employees, "You must prove to me that your idea merits consideration," they must learn to say, "We will find a way to implement your suggestion unless there is some very good reason not to and we will be accountable for proving why not."

This idea encounters considerable resistance from managers. They often feel that this is sort of a Pandora's box. Yet this part of the process is the key to establishing management credibility. There are really no workable alternatives. No amount of reorganization, training, incentives, or changes in personnel will function as a substitute. Without management credibility, it is naive to believe that enough members of the workforce will be willing to expend the extraordinary effort required to produce breakthroughs in performance.

PART OF THE ROUTINE

Several weeks after the initiation of the employee involvement teams, the groups will begin to settle into a fairly regular weekly routine. Once the first list of issues is documented and assigned and the team selects a problem to work on, the weekly agenda becomes more consistent. A typical one hour team meeting might include the following activities:

- Agree on day's agenda—three minutes.
- Review Team Action Register—fifteen minutes.
  Status of open issues
  Assign new actions
  Close completed issues
- List new issues—ten minutes.
  Identify and clarify
  Assign priority
  Determine responsibility
- Work on team problem—thirty minutes.
  Problem-solving steps

- Set agenda for next meeting—two minutes.

This routine is not rigid, of course, as meetings often involve bridge team members visiting to discuss issues, special training in problem-solving techniques, critical issues that require more extensive time, and the like, but it gives you a general idea of how much time each team should devote to each segment.

One segment that should always be afforded enough time, however, is the team problem. If the team does not set aside a regular block of time to work on it and spends too much time discussing action item issues, the team will soon become frustrated with how long it takes to work through the problem-solving process. Sufficient time for working the problem-solving process must be allocated each week, either during the team meeting or at other times during the week, so the team maintains a sense of steady progress.

Teams are a part of the growth of an employee involvement process and the growth of the company, and, most importantly, the employees. While employees may be standoffish and hesitant at first, they will soon warm to their responsibilities when it becomes clear that they are indeed making a difference.

CHAPTER SIX

TRACKING SUCCESS

In Chapter Two, we touched upon the importance of measurement as a key element of the employee involvement process. Measurement is important both from a bottom line productivity improvement standpoint and as a factor in assessing the effectiveness of the organizational change intervention.

There are a number of principles related to the measurement process that should be considered.

MEASURE IT AND
PERFORMANCE IMPROVES

At first, this may sound almost magical. How can simply measuring some aspect of performance result in an improvement? The key lies in the fact that the measurement process itself causes a heightened awareness of the phenomenon being measured. As people pay more attention to the measured item, consciously and subconsciously they do things that result in better performance.

Take, for instance, our friends at Finley, where one operation involved the insertion of integrated circuits into a template that would later be used during circuit board assembly. Many components were being placed in the wrong location or were misoriented on the template. A team member began posting the daily errors found at inspection in the work area next to the insertion stations. Within three weeks the number of errors dropped by two-thirds, with no change in the process. The only difference was that the operators could now "see" the errors coming out of their area.

Obviously, there is more to it than this. There must be an ability to change. For example, measuring the performance of a machine will not cause the machine to improve on its own. The operator running the machine or technician maintaining it, however, can see the performance measurements and frequently make necessary adjustments. Another important requirement is that the measurements must be both seen and understood by those people who can directly impact the performance being measured. This leads to the second principle.

MEASUREMENTS MUST BE VISIBLE

In America's corporate world, it's not unusual to see managers, supervisors, quality control inspectors, cost analysts, and others wave reams of measurement reports in the air and complain that the backlog is increasing, the quality trend is down, or costs are out of line. When asked if the people doing the work are aware of this, their response often is, "Well, they ought to be, they're the ones causing the problem," or "Sure they are! I told them our quality was going to hell at our informative meeting last month and nothing's changed." **An army of analysts, statisticians, and chart makers in your company pumping out stacks of performance reports are useless**

unless this information gets back to the people who are directly responsible for doing the work.

Simply mounting a large bulletin board in the work area, posting several key performance measurement charts, and having the area supervisor or manager gather the employees in front of the board on a regular basis to explain the results and identify specific performance concerns achieves remarkable results. This, however, leads to two more principles of measurement.

MEASUREMENTS MUST BE MEANINGFUL

It is important to know the intent of the information before presenting performance results to employees. If the purpose is merely to inform them of the results, then the timing and content of the feedback is not so critical. For example, a manager may hold a quarterly or semiannual meeting to share plantwide performance data and major issues facing the company. It is naive, however, to think these kinds of meetings will have an impact on future performance. They are a necessary part of keeping people informed of the general business situation, but do little to change behaviors. The kind of measurements that affect behavior and performance are those that relate directly to the individual or the immediate work group. For instance, compare the following two feedback statements:

> "The quarterly yield of our combined production lines last month was 92 percent. We need to do better."

> "Frank, the first pass yield off your machine yesterday was 92 percent against an area

> average of 98 percent. The defects were primarily missing components, so be sure to watch your supply tubes."

Needing, or wanting to "do better" often leads only to frustration and misdirected activity unless the measurement systems are providing meaningful information that can be easily understood and acted upon by the people doing the work.

One way of checking to make sure that measurements are meaningful is to ask people to explain the reports or charts. It is amazing how often, when asked to explain a performance graph posted in the work area, people will respond:

> "Beats me! The quality guy just comes down here every month and updates it."

> "Labor variance? I'm not sure. I think it has something to do with our efficiency."

> "That chart tells us how many widgets we produced last month. How many are we supposed to produce this month? Gee, I don't know, they don't tell us that."

Sometimes the sheer quantity of information is overwhelming. The computer age has made it possible to gather and analyze a tremendous amount of data. Management Information System (MIS) departments have been established to create sophisticated data collection and reporting systems. Giant computers spew out thousands of pages of measurement reports that inundate managers daily. A manager sitting at a desk stacked six inches high with computer printouts might say:

"This report tells me every operation performed in my area last week, the efficiency at each station, what jobs were run, who ran them, when they were run, how many parts were produced, etc, etc, etc."

"What do I do with the report? Oh, it sits here until I get next week's report, then I throw it away."

"Do I use it to help run my shop? No, not really. It's broken down into so much detail that it doesn't really give me anything I can use, like operation summaries, trends, critical elements out of line, and the like. I just keep it around in case my boss asks me about it."

MIS contributions to the business world are many. Computer applications have been responsible for significant increases in productivity and the ability to process a greater amount of information in a shorter period of time. But these systems must be used wisely and constantly checked to make sure that the measurement and feedback reports are of practical use to the recipients. Otherwise they'll most likely get dumped into recycling bins to help defray the high cost of paper usage.

FEEDBACK MUST BE TIMELY

By now, it's easy to see that, for a measurement system to work as a performance improvement mechanism, the data generated by the system must also be fed back in a timely manner. It seems that the ability to make productive performance changes is inversely proportional to the time it takes to receive feedback about that performance. In other words, if production workers find out that a device assembled two weeks ago had a miswire in it, they probably won't remember it, and almost certainly won't recall the circumstances surrounding the operation at that time in order to assess why the error might have occurred. On the other hand, if the feedback was received the next day, or better yet, the same day, immediate corrective action could be taken.

Real-time feedback is sometimes very difficult, if not impossible, to achieve in some operations. Processes like plating and software development, for instance, can't be tested until an entire series of steps are complete. It is equally important, however, for managers to understand in such cases that they can't expect too much positive change when the feedback is delayed very long. The degree to which a real-time environment is achieved determines the degree of control over this aspect of the operation.

EXPECTATIONS MUST BE CLEAR

The last important element necessary to maximize the effectiveness of a measurement system is performance expectations or goals. Measurements and feedback are of limited value unless they are put into the context of desired outcomes and results. For every measurement there should be a goal or standard toward which people are working. Again, compare the following scenarios:

> "Our output last week was 240 widgets. We've got to do better than that if we think we're going to get caught up."

"I didn't know we were behind."

"We sure are. Shipping calls me every day saying they need more parts."

"How many do they need?"

"I don't know, but it's a lot."

"Well, how many should we be making each week if 240 isn't enough?"

"How am I supposed to know? Just make as many as you can and maybe shipping will get off our backs."

"Our output last week was 240 widgets against a goal of 260. The goal was set to meet a weekly demand of 230 parts plus reduce a backlog of ninety widgets over the next three weeks. So, we met this week's demand, but only managed to reduce the backlog by ten instead of thirty as planned."

"Are we still trying to eliminate the backlog in three weeks?"

"Yes, but it now means we have to produce an extra forty-five parts each week. That makes this week's goal 275 widgets. You think you can handle it?"

"We would have made the 260 if the number two press hadn't gone down Thursday. It's running fine now, so I think we can do it, although we might need to work a few hours overtime."

"OK. Let's see where we stand at the end of

each day against a target of fifty-five widgets per day. That will give us the 275 we need by the end of the week. As a challenge, if we can make the goal without overtime, the coffee and doughnuts are on me next Monday!"

"You're on! Let's do it!"

This may sound awfully simple. It is. But it is also surprising how many employees don't know what is expected of them or their work unit on a daily or weekly basis.

MEASURE WHAT'S HAPPENING NOW

While results-oriented measurements remain important, process-oriented indicators provide the most powerful information. Coupled with proper process analysis, training, and authorization, techniques such as statistical process control will allow employees to identify trends that might produce defects. The ability to anticipate when a process is about to go out of control allows employees to stop **before** defects occur and take appropriate preventive actions. While measurements are handy for determining how well something was done, it is clearly more effective to determine how well you are **doing**.

The absence of such indicators is roughly equivalent to driving a car by looking only at the rearview mirror. You know where you've been, but you haven't a clue about the big rock in the road just ahead. In some companies, the use of measurement is even worse. To strain this metaphor a bit further, the existing corporate environment might be described as one in which the driver of the car (in other words, the person who actually does the work) is blindfolded. The manager is in the back seat looking out the rear window yelling orders at the driver. Often then, after the crash, the worker gets the ticket and has his or her insurance canceled. How much smarter it is to take the blindfold off! The manager's job, then, is to look at the map and decide whether to go to Las Vegas or Chicago.

INVOLVE THE CUSTOMER

In addition to the ultimate consumer of the product or service, all members of the organization have their own customers. All tasks have inputs, processes, and outputs. The person or group who uses the output is, in a very real way, a customer. Software designers write programs used by test technicians. Engineers create technical drawings used by other engineers and assembly workers. Managers devise schedules used by supervisors, workers, and other managers. These internal customers are the ones who best know if these internal products and services meet their needs.

Simple indicators are often the best. Again, it is prudent to design these measures as process indicators. Rather than completing the product and asking, "How did I do?," it is far better to check along the way and ask, "How am I doing? If I keep doing what I'm doing will it work for you? If I make this change will it help?" For instance, a manufacturing engineer writing assembly instructions might meet periodically with the assemblers and assess progress. Or a trainer might meet periodically with the participants to see if the material and exercises will meet their needs.

Although manufacturing and production examples have been used in most of the measurement discussion, goals and expectations are equally important in other functions. White collar jobs may be more difficult to measure on a daily basis, but the principle is just as relevant. Staff employees need to set goals and know what is expected of them on their jobs. They should be able to describe these expectations when asked, and should receive timely feedback about progress toward goals more often than the annual performance review.

The measurement system used in white collar areas may vary widely depending upon the particular function involved, but the process used to determine the measurements is fairly common. It basically consists of the leaders in the area sitting down with the individuals and small groups of workers and customers to decide what kinds of measurements make sense for their specific jobs or functions. For example, software developers may want to have a measurement based upon the number of lines of good code written. Hardware designers may decide to measure themselves against a development timetable. Financial analysts might monitor the accuracy and timeliness of their reports. Human relations workers could use a client service satisfaction assessment as a measure of their performance.

But determining the measurements themselves is not necessarily the most important aspect of the process. The real key lies in the discussion and negotiation of the measurements between manager, customer, and subordinates. It is this negotiation process that clarifies everyone's expectations and needs for all involved, as well as what will be required to accomplish the agreed-upon goals.

Often the goals are very difficult to measure accurately on a strictly objective basis, for example the level of service provided by a maintenance organization. It may be easy to agree upon the desire to provide a "high level of service to maintain satisfied customers." Where numerical measurements cannot be defined, however, it becomes even more important for the manager or client to give immediate feedback to the subordinate or service organization if there is even a **feeling** of less-than-satisfactory performance. This feeling is just as important a measurement as numerical data. By openly discussing the discomfort with the performance, each party is able to better grasp the expectations and resolve conflicts before they escalate.

Unfortunately, in case after case, employees receive poor annual or semiannual performance reviews for not measuring up to the manager's expectations, yet aren't aware of the problems until the appraisal discussion. Managers often comment, "He could have done better," or "She was just doing enough to get by," or "I just didn't feel like he was accomplishing everything we had agreed to at the beginning of the year." When asked about the feedback the employee had been given during the year, the manager would respond, "Well, it was never anything I could really put my finger on. He was doing his job, but I never felt like he was giving it his all. I never talked to him about it because I kept thinking he would pull out of it on his own and do better."

It is exactly this "feeling" we're talking about. It's quite similar, in fact, to the situation in Chapter Two, in which we discussed how employees who are told simply to "work harder" aren't able to increase productivity nearly as much as those who know specifically what they need to improve on or do. In white collar jobs, the way performance is perceived by the manager or the customer is often a very subjective yet valid and important measure of the worker. The employee needs and deserves feedback of these subjective measures just as much as the more objective, numerical standards. The feedback can be given on a very informal basis, as simple as a one-on-one or one-to-group discussion with an open expression of feelings about the performance and what is expected. The manager must also be willing to listen carefully to the subordinates' response to the feedback.

Occasionally there are circumstances that have changed since the goals were established, making the original expectations unrealistic. An open dialogue will clear the air and allow new or revised goals to be set. It is this continual process of goal negotiation and clarification that keeps people on track, in line with the latest business needs and priorities, and in harmony with one another. When the annual performance review time rolls around, the appraisal simply becomes a formal documentation of the employee's performance during the year and meets the number one criterion of an appraisal: "no surprises."

THE PROCESS YARDSTICK

Up to this point the focus has been upon measurement as an assessment of the performance of an individual or work unit toward meeting business objectives and using measurement systems to improve organizational performance. But this book also looks at the "big picture" of organizational change and the implementation of new and different management processes. How does an organization assess whether or not the change process is achieving the desired results? Obviously, bottom line, productivity trends (efficiency, quality, unit costs, scrap, schedule attainment, etc.) are important measures of the success of the change effort.

Optimum organizational effectiveness can only be achieved, however, when all ten elements of the employee involvement model are in balance with one another. So how do you know if the change intervention has made a positive impact on leadership, people development, reward, or work setting? Has a short term improvement in unit cost been achieved at the expense of long-term quality improvement? How are people perceiving the recent changes? Answering these kinds of questions is what is meant by measuring the success of the total **process**. The remainder of this chapter will examine how to develop this important aspect of measurement.

Beyond these fundamental business performance measures are indicators that permit monitoring of the progress of the employee involvement process itself. Depending upon the size, complexity, and the number and gravity of problems within the organization, meaningful improvements in the performance indicators may not appear for months or even years from the initiation of the employee involvement process. It is important to develop independent measurements that indicate if the right things are happening along the way. An ongoing assessment will allow you to anticipate problems and make appropriate adjustments before the process is damaged.

In employee involvement process measurements, there are four broad categories:

- Attitude surveys
- Informal reports
- Accountability tracking, and
- Activity metrics.

Attitude Surveys

There are always some issues people are reluctant to discuss openly, especially in the very early stages of the EI process. At least one component of the overall assessment effort must permit anonymous input. We designed and use a 108 item survey in many major projects. It contains eight to twelve rating scales related to each of the ten elements of the model described in Chapter Two. A sampling of these items may be found in Appendix B. Before the employee involvement process begins, every employee is surveyed to establish a baseline for comparison over time. This anonymous survey is then repeated every three to six months. As the averages within each category are plotted and examined, trends become apparent. To understand the meaning of these trends, the survey results are shared with the members of the core group, who then make recommendations for modifications of the process.

In one organization, a follow-up survey showed improvements in four categories, no change in four other categories, and declines in the leadership and reward categories. These results were reported to all employees—a requirement for any survey. Then the core group was asked to review the results and make recommendations for improvements. The essence of their conclusions was that the reward decline was due to a perceived inequity: employees felt they were working harder and achieving improvements, but weren't being recognized for their extra effort. They attributed the decline in the leadership category to the managers' poor communication skills.

Now that they had isolated the problems, the next step was to decide what to do about them. The core group designed a series of recognition events including barbecues and pizza parties and the managers received *Leader Effectveness Training* (1977), an intensive communication skill development workshop.

There is really no substitute for such surveys. It is essential to have an assessment device that allows all employees to express their opinions without fear of retribution.

Several important principles are at stake with the use of surveys:

- The survey must adhere to scientific requirements in design, analysis, and interpretation of the resulting data.

- The survey should be administered by professionals with no stake in the outcome.

- Individual confidentiality must be preserved.

- The results are the property of the participants and must be revealed in full to all participants immediately upon completion of the data analysis.

- Participants have the right to influence the interpretation of the data analysis.

- Participants have the right to influence the use of the resulting information and make recommendations for action.

- Recommended actions should be completed

swiftly and thoroughly.

Informal Reports

Although surveys provide crucial information that cannot be obtained any other way, they can't do the whole job. Surveys are slow, give only the information specifically requested, and lack richness of detail. They do serve as important anchors that prevent wild speculation and imprudent risks, but organizations are dynamic and fast-paced and therefore also require some gut-level indicators.

Checklists, feedback cards, sensing sessions, facilitator reports, management presentations, and other quick and simple information gathering techniques should be pursued vigorously by the bridge team. This allows the construction of a continuous, vivid picture of the health of the process. Here, the trick is lots of communication, feedback, and quick responses rather than major detailed plans.

Accountability Tracking

The responsibility for executing the change rests with each and every participant. Those in leadership roles, however, have special responsibilities. If the people who control the resources continue to be measured according to the same criteria used before the initiation of employee involvement, it is unrealistic to expect much progress. Probably the simplest and easiest way to monitor the effectiveness of the organizational leaders is to track the number of employee suggestions implemented. Now that's not the number of suggestions received, not the magnitude of the suggestions, but the number implemented. The power of this comes from a reversal of the burden of proof.

One of the most serious shortcomings of quality circles as used in the United States is the lack of managers' accountability to employees. In the typical quality circles program, employees or teams of employees would submit recommendations to management. Managers then evaluate the suggestions. If employees can prove a suggestion will reduce cost or improve performance, it may be approved. If not, it is rejected. The burden of proof, obviously, is on the employees. Since the teams had only limited time, resources, and skills, only a very few recommendations could qualify. In a very short time, employees become disillusioned and quit trying.

The reversal of this suggests that managers make every effort to implement employee suggestions unless there is some very good reason not to. The burden of proof must rest with management. This allows senior managers to detect leadership problems within the organization. A manager or supervisor with a low percentage of implemented suggestions may need additional resources or development. Leaders who have chronic difficulty implementing suggestions should perhaps be moved to a nonleadership role. This sort of accountability tracking should ultimately be incorporated into the normal management performance review process.

The typical resistance to this type of accountability are the fears that "stupid" ideas will be implemented and that it undermines the manager's authority. Neither of these fears is justified. The manager retains the authority to turn down any suggestion that is contrary to the principles outlined in the vision or is clearly contrary to the needs of the business. If a large number of the suggestions seem unproductive, it probably means that some element of the employee involvement process has been neglected. Perhaps the employees have been given insufficient information about the business. Perhaps conflicts within the unit have gone unresolved. Perhaps the manager has failed to master the necessary skills. In any case, it is a clear signal that a leadership problem exists, a signal raised by this very valuable accountability tracking.

Activity Metrics

To make progress, many activities need to occur—teams are formed, training is provided, meetings are held, presentations are made. Tracking and reporting such things as the percentage of employees on teams, the number of management presentations given, the hours invested in training, etc., are common activity metrics. While it is important to systematically keep track of this kind of information, some organizations are lulled into thinking that activity equals progress. Many change projects involve great flurries of activity, but when the dust settles nothing has really changed. This is why the other kinds of measures mentioned previously are significantly better indicators of true change progress.

As you can see, these measurement tools allow all of the people in the system to maintain a realistic perspective on the organization and the change process. Knowledge is power here, and the knowledge and therefore the power is shared by all.

CHAPTER SEVEN

HOLDING THE FUTURE
IN YOUR HANDS

Simply choosing to initiate a change process exhibits great strength, foresight, and commitment. A company may not have descended into pandemonium, but someone has seen the need for stemming the madness and acted upon it. When we discussed the meaning of madness in our introduction, the fourth definition actually indicated the sort of elation employees and managers feel when things begin to work the way everyone had hoped they could.

WILD EXCITEMENT OR ENTHUSIASM
There are innumerable examples of companies that have swapped one sort of "corporate madness" for another, more pleasant sort:

At Motorola, a troubled pager business shows so much improvement in quality and effectiveness that it became a major supplier to one of the most demanding Japanese customers. Quality is so good that rework and scrap have almost disappeared. At their cellular phone factory, quality is so high that retail dealers and distributors have been instructed to give a new phone to any customer who brings in a defective one. Motorola was the first major corporation to win the newly developed Malcolm Baldridge Award, the country's highest honor for quality improvement.

Florida Power & Light wins the Deming Prize, awarded by the Japanese government to companies that excel in quality and excellence in service and products. Until only a few years before, the Deming Prize was an honor reserved only for the finest companies in Japan.

With the help of companywide employee involvement teams, Ford outearns General Motors two years running and rewards its employees with a fat bonus.

Members of an employee involvement team at Intel change their job title from "janitor" to "floor manager." After investigating various ways to improve productivity, they recommend the purchase of a $6,000 floor cleaning machine. With it, they are able to improve productivity enough to complete their own work in half the time and bid jobs at nearby facilities for half what was being paid to outside contractors.

At a Honeywell circuit board factory, one key event seemed to trigger an avalanche of record-setting achievements. Two operators who worked together as a team on a circuit pattern exposure machine (printer) set a one-day goal of 800 panels. The documented standard for an eight-hour shift was just under 600 panels. Spelling each other during breaks and cutting short their lunch period, the two women print 806 panels during a single shift. They drew a large "happy face" on a piece of newsprint, scribbled the words "We did it!—806 Panels!," and taped it to the window of their room. The next day, signs began springing up all over the building as other operators began establishing goals and setting new records on their own jobs.

At another Honeywell factory, a new avionics product is developed and brought to market. With the help of what they called Total Involvement of People, the new division is making money well in advance of company expectations.

All of these are examples of actual companies that have taken their futures into their own hands. Most of this book has focused on organizations that are or have been entrenched in traditional, hierarchical management systems and now want to achieve higher levels of performance and improved quality of worklife for their people. By now, you can see how this process permits great strides toward optimizing all aspects of the organization by unleashing the creative potential within all people and channeling it toward the attainment of a common vision.

As professional change agents, we have personally observed and shared in the feelings of excitement, accomplishment, and pride as organizations have implemented employee involvement and achieved outstanding improvements in performance and job satisfaction. A word of caution is appropriate, however. Starting the employee involvement process is indeed like dancing with the bear: once you start, you can't stop if you get tired yet your partner wants to continue. This is true even when the initial vision's goals have been achieved. Complacency is the enemy. Employee involvement is a people development process and productivity improvement is an outcome. The people development element stresses the importance of new learning and constant growth. If you're not growing, you're dying! It's just that simple.

The good news is that there are countless opportunities for continued growth and improvement. If it is true that the only **constant** in the universe is **change**, then as you reach what was once the future desired state, it becomes the present state upon which to develop a new future vision. The continued repetition of this cycle is called renewal, and it is a long-term commitment by the organization to continuous self examination and improvement. There are many opportunities to take the basic foundation provided by employee involvement and carry it into the future to achieve even higher levels of performance in the face of new social trends, international competition in the world market, and the increasing rate of technological innovation.

BACK TO BASICS

In many schools and businesses, people have lost sight of the few, simple, and fundamental elements required for achieving success. In our zeal to meet the challenge of increasing complexity and rapid change, we have created management systems that have added to the complexity and distracted us from paying attention to those things that really count. Fortunately, amid our turned on, high tech, fast-lane society, we are seeing an encouraging phenomenon:

a trend "back to the basics."

In their introduction to *A Passion for Excellence* (1985), Tom Peters and Nancy Austin sum up the "back to basics" revolution this way:

> "The basics got lost in a blur of well-meaning gibberish that took us further and further from excellent performance in any sphere. We got so tied up in our techniques, devices, and programs that we forgot about people—the people who produce the product or service and the people who consume it."

Peters and Austin go on to identify several of the basics of managerial success, although they are quick to point out that they won't be found in the leading management textbooks. Some of these basics include pride in the organization and enthusiasm for its works, "naive" listening to customers, customer perception of services and quality, employee commitment and ownership, fostering innovation and internal entrepreneurship, trust, vision, and leadership.

To this, we add our hearty "Amen!" The employee involvement process described in this book provides an avenue for an organization to break free from the bureaucratic shackles that have forced it to lose sight of the key ingredients of success. It is one thing to read through the list of basics and say, "Well, of course. Those are just common sense things we all ought to be doing." It is not quite so simple, however, when starting with an organization that has low trust, a vague vision, alienated employees, marginal quality, and dissatisfied customers. The steps we have outlined will go a long way toward "getting back to the basics" and achieving excellent performance and business success.

WHERE TO NOW?

Once these initial objectives have been met, what next? How do you sustain the enthusiasm and begin the renewal process? There are some advanced applications of employee involvement that lead to the next plateau. Of course, these are not appropriate until **after** an acceptable level of success based on the ten model elements has already been achieved. (The exception to this caveat is in a new start-up operation, where these concepts can be incorporated from the very beginning.)

SEMI-AUTONOMOUS WORK GROUPS

There are three fundamental aspects of work:
- Planning it
- Controlling it, and
- Doing it.

Traditionally, the responsibility for these tasks has been segmented and assigned to different groups of people: engineers or staff groups do the planning; managers do the controlling; and operators do the "doing." On the surface, this separation and specialization appears to make sense—divide a complex task into parts and assign specialized experts to focus on their individual areas of responsibility. Unfortunately, this approach often has disturbing consequences. The more a task is divided into pieces, the less ownership and responsibility people feel for the outcome of the task. In addition, the more a task is broken into simple, repetitive elements, the less motivated, challenged, and satisfied people feel about their work. So any productivity gains that might have been realized through simplification and specialization are typically more than offset by alienation of the workforce.

The employee involvement process, on the other hand, encourages people to take on more responsibility for their jobs, learn more about the business, and have more control over their work. A natural evolution of the team process is to build the EI team structure right into the structure of the job itself and to form semiautonomous (or self-managing) work teams. These teams have a much greater control over all three aspects of their work and may have responsibility for such things as:

- Daily work assignments
- Job planning and scheduling
- Time and record-keeping
- Tool and supply ordering
- Budgeting and expense control
- Team goal setting
- Team member selection
- Resolving internal conflicts
- Quality control
- Training of members
- Problem solving
- Routine maintenance
- Member discipline
- Performance appraisal
- Promotional readiness

The key criteria for forming semiautonomous teams include:

- Clear accountability for a whole task
- A common goal (i.e., a team product or service)
- Interdependence of group members (i.e., they need each to reach their goal)
- Multiple skills (not just multiple tasks) on each team
- Team size limited to a maximum of twelve members.

Each team has complete responsibility for all aspects of some clearly defined and measurable whole task. This could be the complete assembly, inspection, and test of a given product (or a major subassembly of a large, complex product), or possibly the operation of one section of a large production process area. The team shares a common goal and its success is measured against the entire team's ability to achieve this goal within pre-established parameters. The defined task is such that multiple skills are required to complete it successfully and there is a high degree of interdependence among the members of the group. Quite often a skill-based pay system or a "pay-for-knowledge" plan is used in conjunction with the team structure to encourage members to learn a variety of skills. This gives the team greater flexibility in work assignments and enables individual members to rotate jobs to relieve fatigue, eyestrain, or the sheer monotony of doing a particular task for an extended period of time, and to provide coverage in case of absence due to illness or vacation. The team is kept small (eight to twelve members) to allow effective, face-to-face meetings for decision-making and coordination of tasks.

The leadership role changes dramatically when converting to a semiautonomous work team concept. The traditional first-line supervisor function is no longer necessary or appropriate. This person is replaced by a "team leader" or "coordinator" who is selected by the team and whose main function is to serve as the primary communication link within the team, with management, and with other teams. The role is often rotated among group members, with each person serving for a designated period of time. In a skill-based pay organization, the team coordinator role is just one more set of skills that can be acquired by team members, and a person's pay reflects the attainment of this skill level.

Management's role also changes in a self-managing environment. The manager now holds the **team** accountable for goal attainment and operating results, whereas the team is responsible for holding its members accountable for individual performance. This second-level manager's title often changes to team "advisor," "facilitator," or some similar designation. It is his or her role to work within the organizational system to see that the teams are provided with the information and resources they need to successfully perform their tasks.

The evolution from employee involvement teams to semiautonomous work groups can bring about another significant improvement in organizational effectiveness and quality of worklife. From a business standpoint, benefits include improved productivity, higher quality, reduced overhead (with less surveillance required), and fewer internal conflicts. From the employees' viewpoint, the process provides an opportunity to exercise more control over many aspects of daily worklife. Stronger feelings of ownership and commitment to company and team goals emerge as the teams begin to experience the sensation of "running their own business."

Just as teams can pave the way for a more advanced concept, so should rewards evolve.

GAINSHARING/EMPLOYEE OWNERSHIP

Reward and recognition are important for improving and sustaining performance and job satisfaction. Many productivity improvement plans are based upon monetary incentives such as gainsharing, profit sharing, piecework incentives, and the like. Financial reward alone, however, will not generate long-term productivity gains. Those organizations that have also focused on the other elements of Total Employee Involvement can achieve sustained improvements with financial reward systems, but the two must go hand in hand. As an organization demonstrates significant performance increases through employee involvement or self-managing teams, it is only fair and just to share some of the financial gains with the employees.

There are several types of reward systems that can do this equitably and achieve the desired results. Gainsharing, profit sharing, bonuses, or other special perquisites are all viable options. Tangible rewards should be planned and given on several different levels. First, there should be individual merit rewards given by the teams to fellow members based upon individual performance. This might be an annual merit increase that is part of the normal salary plan. Second, there should be team rewards given by management that are based upon the team achieving its goals and objectives. This could be a gainsharing plan that returns a percentage of the improvements attained by the team during the past quarter or year. Team members share equally in this reward. Finally, there should be a plantwide reward plan based upon total plant performance. Here, a profit sharing system may be a good approach for returning a portion of the plant's net profit to all contributing employees.

Some organizations have incorporated direct employee ownership as part of the process. As major stockholders in the company, the words "ownership" and "commitment" take on new and even greater significance than before. Companies like Worthington Steel and America West Airlines have built stock ownership right into the employment requirements in the hope that the motivation for shared profits will result in stronger commitment and better customer service.

Other companies have used employee ownership as a last-ditch effort to keep their organization from going out of business. Rather than closing the doors and laying everyone off, employees have rallied to the cause by investing their own money in the plant and placing their destiny in their own hands. This has often led to dramatic turnarounds in a company's performance. The reason is quite simple. **People will work harder for and remain committed to something they have a direct personal stake in than they will for some faceless stockholder who couldn't care less about the organization as long as quarterly dividends are being paid.**

INTRAPRENEURSHIP

In many cases, especially in large, established corporations, employee ownership may not be possible or practical. A viable alternative being tried in several companies today is "intrapreneuring," a concept made popular by Gifford Pinchot III in his book (1985) of the same name. The term, coined by Pinchot, refers to "intracorporate entrepreneurship," a process whereby a person or group inside a large organization is given the resources and support to develop and produce a new or improved product or service. The concept attempts to create entrepreneurial conditions—autonomy, control over resources, freedom to experiment and pursue a subject of personal interest—within the corporate structure. The objective is to harness each individual's creativity and drive and direct it toward the pursuit of a goal that will benefit both the person and the company. Typically, intrapreneurial ventures involve a fairly small percentage of the population and are not part of the mainstream business activity, so this process has limited application. It does work very well, however, in organizations that need to develop new products quickly or where the work can be broken down into smaller, somewhat independent projects.

THE FINLEY STORY—PHASE II

The scenarios we have described may seem too utopian to be put into practice, but, in fact, this is exactly what is occurring in many progressive organizations around the country and what has evolved at Finley. After a few years of success with the employee involvement process, Finley reached a plateau. All the performance measures remained very high and the people of Finley were quite proud of their accomplishments, but the energy level was dropping and fewer and fewer ideas were being raised in team meetings. It became evident that a renewal process was required to maintain the spirit of challenge and enthusiasm.

About this same time, Finley was being considered as the site for production of the circuit boards for a new, advanced technology computer. These boards would be more complex than Finley's existing product, and would require radical new manufacturing processes and technology. It also meant that the people involved in the production operation would have to be extremely committed to the highest standards of process and quality control. Because of Finley's previous success, it was indeed selected as the site for the new operation.

The decision to change the technical mission of Finley also provided a perfect opportunity to examine the entire sociotechnical system and incorporate an organizational renewal process at the same time. The steering committee and change agents established a planning team comprised of engineers, managers, operators, personnel specialists, and internal organization development consultants. The core group responded with a revised manifesto, adding:

- Commitment to honesty, integrity, and trust
- Personal and team responsibility and accountability
- Leadership as part of everyone's job
- Peer feedback and control, and
- Commitment to team goals.

The organization was also restructured around semiautonomous work teams called "small business partnerships." The name is appropriate since each partnership team is responsible for managing the daily affairs of their assigned portion of the production process (with duties similar to those described in the previous section). The term also helps promote and reinforce a spirit of ownership and commitment to their team and the organization.

The production workforce—now called "associates"—were converted to an all-salaried structure and people are now paid for knowledge and performance rather than the former fixed job rate. The knowledge pay is based upon learning each of the skills required for the assigned partnership. As each new skill is mastered—based upon a predetermined set of performance criteria—an associate's base pay is adjusted upward. In addition, the salary also includes a merit amount based upon job performance.

Each partnership selected its own team coordinator. This leadership position is one of the skill sets on each team, and, as mentioned earlier, is primarily a coordination and communication role. All major team decisions are made by the team using a consensus process.

The structure and role of management and the technical support groups also changed as a result of Phase II. Finley management consists of three managers (operations, engineering, and quality) who oversee the partnership activities. Their primary role is to establish overall business objectives and product standards, maintain the code of conduct, define the partnership teams' decision space, and, if necessary, facilitate conflict resolution.

The Finley technical team (engineers, maintenance technicians, lab technicians) acts in a supporting role to the small business partnerships. This group is responsible for establishing the process and product quality parameters, developing cost standards, installing equipment and facilities, performing major troubleshooting and maintenance, developing new processes, and serving as problem-solving consultants to the teams. By allowing the partnerships to run the day-to-day activities of the factory, management and engineering departments are free to focus on major production issues, long range planning, technology enhancements, and new business opportunities.

Of course, this change did not come about overnight. Much time and effort went into the planning and execution of each step of the transformation. Two steps of the change plan are especially noteworthy. Even though Finley personnel already felt a high degree of job responsibility and ownership, the small business partnership concept demanded a significantly higher level of accountability from every associate. Knowing that this would be the case, for Phase II the entire Finley workforce was built from scratch. Everyone was given the opportunity to decide whether they wanted to be part of the new operation. If they did, they submitted an application and participated in a selection process that assessed work history, knowledge and ability, motivation and interest, teamwork, integrity, responsibility, leadership, participation, and innovation. All candidates were given clear expectations about the behavior and values necessary to succeed in the new environment. Not all existing Finley employees chose to participate, and some who did apply were not selected, often because of an unwillingness to learn multiple skills or take on leadership responsibilities.

The select group then embarked on the next step of the change plan: intensive education and training. The Finley facility was shut down for several months while it was renovated and re-equipped for the new operations. This afforded an ideal opportunity to conduct much of the necessary "nonproduction" training.

Required for all Finley personnel, the training and education program focused on three major areas: social and interpersonal skills; technical knowledge and skills; and organizational knowledge and skills. In total, this training required almost nine full weeks of classroom time. With the Finley facility closed down, the courses were scheduled so that people worked at their jobs in another company facility approximately half the time, and devoted the other half to the training.

The classroom experience had several side benefits in addition to the specific course objectives. The courses allowed people to begin establishing relationships in their newly structured partnership teams, where many questions, issues, and concerns about the new operation were addressed and resolved. People were also able to get a feel for the expanded responsibility of their new roles and a broader view of the overall business objectives and vision for the "new Finley." Although intrapreneuring was not suited to their product, partnership members later also received entrepreneur training to help them think creatively like small-business people.

The importance of these initial education and training sessions cannot be overemphasized. Although this effort was a significant investment in both time and dollars, it was absolutely necessary for a venture of this magnitude. Even though the Finley workforce was probably quite advanced compared with most factories, the concept of self-managing work groups represented a huge leap forward in additional responsibility and accountability. Even with all this advanced preparation, when the new facility opened and the small business partnerships began functioning, many challenges and issues surfaced. But the foundation had been laid and the structure and processes were in place to address and resolve problems quickly. Without that solid base of trust, involvement, performance, and teamwork Finley had built during the Total Employee Involvement process, though, they probably would not have made it at all.

Once again, you will likely be impatient and want to move the process along more quickly, but experience has shown that if the implementation is forced, the entire process can collapse and the aborted effort will leave people feeling resentful and betrayed. We can't help but think of the patient bricklayer who starts on a level surface, then, brick by brick, lays the mortar and sets the block. If just one brick is crooked, the entire wall is jeopardized. The bricklayer must then tear down to that level, relay that brick and rebuild. We urge you to move ahead slowly and deliberately, allowing the process to evolve at its own speed. High evolutions like self-managing partnerships are something for every company to look forward to, but not to rush into unprepared.

NO LONGER A CHOICE

American business and industry is caught up in a period of rampant change on many fronts. Fierce competition, both foreign and domestic, has companies scrambling to upgrade technologies, automate outmoded processes, implement advanced information processing capabilities, scale down corporate hierarchies, reduce overhead, and improve product quality and customer service. Social changes have created a more educated—and demanding—

workforce, a higher percentage of working women, increased emphasis on equal opportunity and affirmative action, environmental concerns and a myriad of government regulations.

The question is not whether to change, but **what** has to be changed and **how** to go about it. If a company retreats to its bunker and becomes a victim of the changes around it, its future as an organization is grim. On the other hand, if that company can boldly face change, plan strategy and manage it carefully, it stands a better-than-average chance of coming out a winner.

The American economic system is in a state of **crisis**. The Chinese have an intriguing way of depicting this term, one that fits our current predicament. Their symbol for "crisis" consists of two characters, the first meaning "danger" and the second conveying "hidden opportunity."

CRISIS

———— DANGERS

———— HIDDEN
OPPORTUNITIES

Figure 7-1

As managers and professionals responsible for leading your organizations into the future, you face the same alternatives suggested by these symbols. Either you view the future with fear, expecting dangerous, negative results, or you look forward to the excitement and the challenge, envisioning the positive new opportunities that are waiting to be discovered and harnessed.

Although the problems are very real, the attitude with which you approach them is largely a matter of choice. If you choose to be a leader of change rather than a victim, the concepts and tools described in this book may provide you with a road map to continued success.

Madness? Perhaps! But if it is mad to relish the uncommon dangers and opportunities linked to employee involvement, it is a madness of a different sort.

APPENDIX A

<u>IMPLEMENTATION CHART</u>

At the risk of making all of this seem too easy, we offer a chart that highlights many of the main events that may occur in a major change effort. This chart will help you see the sequence of events and the approximate time required for each phase. Our clients have found this information useful as they develop their employee involvement processes.

Your chart will undoubtedly be quite different. It will be influenced by the size of your organization, the type of business you have, the nature of your production or service process, the number of problems you have, the determination of your competition, the rate of turnover in your workforce, whether you are union or nonunion, your overall financial condition, and many other factors.

The time estimates are very rough. If your organization is relatively small, your workforce stable, your number of problems not excessive, and your financial picture not desperate, you have a reasonable expectation of achieving very good results in about eighteen months. There are, however, no guarantees. It is easy to underestimate how many problems you have or how deep they run, and business conditions can change suddenly. In general, the bigger your company, the more problems you have, the higher your turnover, and the tighter your financial condition, the longer it takes. Three to five years is not unusual.

Some of these factors constitute thresholds. The ideal size for an organization is about 100 people. If you have 200 or 300, you can count on a longer time frame. If your organization is much larger than that, you will probably need to divide it into two or more smaller components. If your turnover is much higher than 4 or 5 percent per year, it is usually wise to bring that into control before proceeding. Even with all of these qualifiers, we nonetheless believe that the chart will be helpful for planning your process.

The chart is divided into five phases. While the activities within each phase are often accomplished in parallel and the sequence will vary considerably, we believe that each major phase should be completed satisfactorily prior to launching the next. The phases correspond roughly to the major phases of the change process: unfreezing, transition, refreezing. Phases I and II are primarily unfreezing. Phases III and IV are mostly transition activities, and Phase V leads you into the refreezing phase.

PHASE I - DEVELOPING SPONSORSHIP AND AWARENESS
3 TO 6 MONTHS

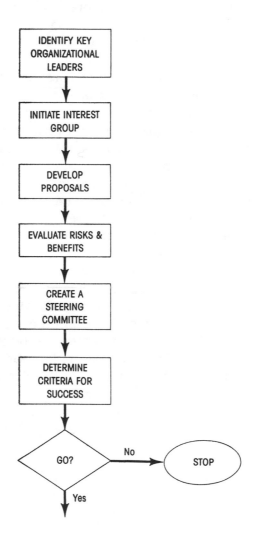

PHASE II - BUILDING COMMITMENT AND PLANNING
3 TO 6 MONTHS

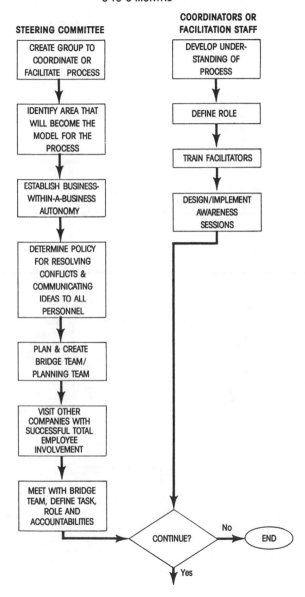

PHASE III - PLANNING
3 TO 6 MONTHS

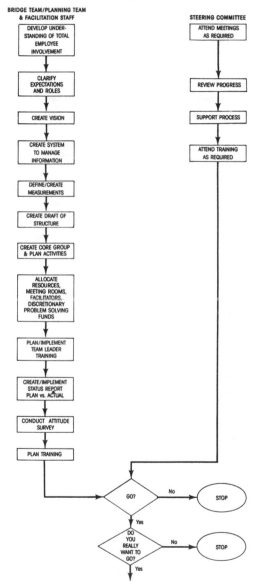

PHASE IV -START UP
2 TO 3 MONTHS

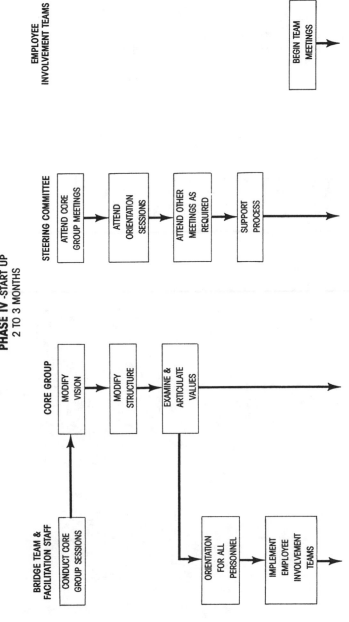

Phase V - ONGOING TASKS
12 - 18 MONTHS TO ∞

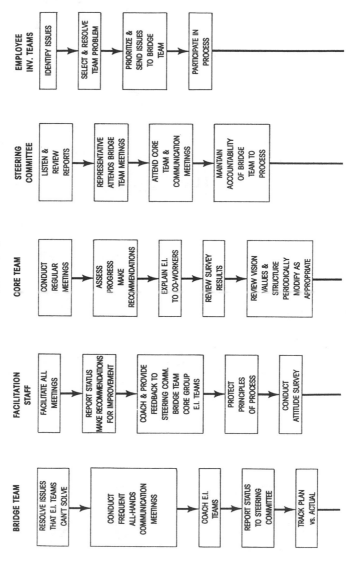

EMPLOYEE INV. TEAMS
- IDENTIFY ISSUES
- SELECT & RESOLVE TEAM PROBLEM
- PRIORITIZE & SEND ISSUES TO BRIDGE TEAM
- PARTICIPATE IN PROCESS

STEERING COMMITTEE
- LISTEN & REVIEW REPORTS
- REPRESENTATIVE ATTENDS BRIDGE TEAM MEETINGS
- ATTEND CORE TEAM & COMMUNICATION MEETINGS
- MAINTAIN ACCOUNTABILITY OF BRIDGE TEAM TO PROCESS

CORE TEAM
- CONDUCT REGULAR MEETINGS
- ASSESS PROGRESS MAKE RECOMMENDATIONS
- EXPLAIN E.I. TO CO-WORKERS
- REVIEW SURVEY RESULTS
- REVIEW VISION VALUES & STRUCTURE PERIODICALLY MODIFY AS APPROPRIATE

FACILITATION STAFF
- FACILITATE ALL MEETINGS
- REPORT STATUS MAKE RECOMMENDATIONS FOR IMPROVEMENT
- COACH & PROVIDE FEEDBACK TO STEERING COMM. BRIDGE TEAM CORE GROUP E.I. TEAMS
- PROTECT PRINCIPLES OF PROCESS
- CONDUCT ATTITUDE SURVEY

BRIDGE TEAM
- RESOLVE ISSUES THAT E.I. TEAMS CAN'T SOLVE
- CONDUCT FREQUENT ALL-HANDS COMMUNICATION MEETINGS
- COACH E.I. TEAMS
- REPORT STATUS TO STEERING COMMITTEE
- TRACK PLAN vs. ACTUAL

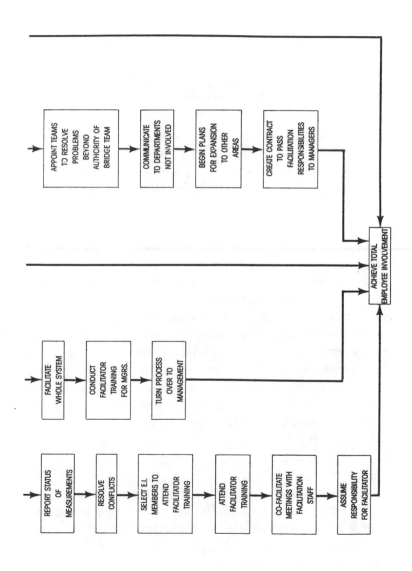

APPENDIX B

ATTITUDE
SURVEY SAMPLING

As mentioned in the text and detailed in Chapter Six, attitude surveys are an important component of assessment. They are an excellent way to gauge employees' perceptions, especially about issues people are reluctant to discuss openly.

Before the employee involvement process begins, every employee is surveyed to establish a baseline for comparison over time. This anonymous survey is then repeated every three to six months. As the averages within each category are plotted and examined, trends become apparent.

We designed and use a 108 item survey in many major projects. It contains eight to twelve rating scales related to each of the ten elements of the model described in Chapter Two. Employees fill out a separate answer sheet to respond to the questions using a five-level scale. A sampling of these items is listed on the next page, with the scale across the top.

A	**B**	**C**	**D**	**E**
STRONGLY DISAGREE	DISAGREE	NEITHER DISAGREE NOR AGREE	AGREE	STRONGLY AGREE

Management almost always follows through in solving problems that we point out to them.

Quality is more important than quantity here.

I receive the proper information about the quality of my work.

I know what the production schedule is.

I help to set the goals which I work toward.

The people in my work group encourage me to work hard.

I have quite a bit of influence about how my job should be done.

I can trust upper management at this plant.

Most of our meetings are productive.

I am given many opportunities to learn new things here.

GLOSSARY

ACTION ITEM: Specific task assigned by a team to an individual member of the team who is responsible for completing it.

BRIDGE TEAM: Cross-functional group composed of plant manager as team leader, each of his/her direct reports, and other important support personnel. Responsible for resolving issues outside the authority of other teams, coordinating plantwide employee involvement activities, and providing leadership for the total process.

CHANGE AGENT: May be called facilitators, coordinators, or consultants. Have as their primary responsibility the overall management of major change efforts within an organization.

CHURN: Excessive rate of employee turnover due to narrowly defined job categories that encourage employees to move from department to department in order to increase wages.

CORE GROUP: A congress of employees, managers, and staff that constitutes a microcosm of the entire organization. All levels, functions, and shifts are represented.

CYBERNETIC SESSION: A technique for gathering a large quantity of ideas from a large group of people in an orderly way.

EMPLOYEE INVOLVEMENT TEAM (EIT): A small group of people (usually six to ten) who performs similar tasks or have a high degree of interdependency that meets on a weekly basis to identify and resolve productivity and quality of worklife problems and issues.

FACILITATOR: May be a change agent. Often is responsible for attending team meetings and providing assistance to the teams and team leaders.

GROUP PROCESS: How a group goes about completing tasks.

INTERVENTION: Any planned activity that causes any member or members of the organization to stop what they are doing and try something different.

LEADERSHIP: One of the ten Total Employee Involvement model elements. The positive behaviors of people occupying leadership roles in the work unit (managers, supervisors, engineers, technical support, group leaders) that create an atmosphere of acceptance, openness, trust, and achievement.

MACHINES: One of the ten Total Employee Involvement model elements. All manufacturing process equipment, including material handling devices, storage systems, computers and terminals, work station tools and fixtures, and office equipment.

MANIFESTO: A document created by the members of the work unit that clearly states the organization's vision and values.

MATERIALS: One of the ten Total Employee Involvement model elements. All direct and indirect materials, shop and office supplies, and vendor supplied parts used in the fabrication or assembly of the product or performance of a service.

MEASUREMENT: One of the ten Total Employee Involvement model elements. The process used to assess the effectiveness of the work being accomplished. Includes measures for individual, group, and work unit performance and a feedback mechanism to communicate results in a timely manner.

METHODS: One of the ten Total Employee Involvement model elements. The operation planning, procedures, documentation, manufacturing processes and management information systems which support the work being done in the organization.

OPINION LEADER: Any person in the organization, at any level, who influences other people's beliefs, feelings, or actions. Usually a vocal representative of the sentiment commonly felt by several other people in the work unit.

PEOPLE DEVELOPMENT: One of the ten Total Employee Involvement model elements. Providing continuous opportunities for training, new learning, career advancement, and work redesign in the work unit.

QUALITY: One of the ten Total Employee Involvement model elements. An ingrained attitude of "do it right the first time" and "errors are avoidable." Having the proper training, capable processes, and necessary tools which allow 100 percent conformance to requirements.

REWARD: One of the ten Total Employee Involvement model elements. The process of providing all members of the work unit adequate and equitable return (both tangible and psychological) for their contributions.

SOCIOTECHNICAL SYSTEM: An organizational construct that demonstrates the inseparable interdependence between the human (social) functions in an organization and the technology used by the organization to perform work.

STEERING COMMITTEE: A management group at the highest level of the organization that establishes policy and strategic direction for Total Employee Involvement.

STRUCTURE: One of the ten Total Employee Involvement model elements. Defines the pattern of communication within the work unit; **who** talks with **whom** about **what** for what **purpose**. Includes all the groups, teams, committees, and formal organization components within the work unit and the communication/feedback systems used to convey information.

TEAM LEADER: Usually the supervisor or manager of the employee involvement team members. Conducts the team meetings and leads the problem-solving and issue resolution processes. Serves as the communication link to the next higher level team in the Total Employee Involvement structure.

TEAM PROBLEM: A problem identified by an employee involvement team that has no readily apparent solution, requires further analysis, needs a team effort to solve, and falls within the team's realm of responsibility. Teams use a structured problem-solving process to arrive at a solution, which is then recommended to management.

WORK SETTING: One of the ten Total Employee Involvement model elements. Includes the physical environment, employee benefits and services, company policies, and practices related to employee work rules.

NOTES

INTRODUCTION

17   Kearney, A.T. "Seeking and Destroying the Wealth Dissipaters." 1985, as quoted in "Miles to Go...or Unity at Last," *Journal for Quality and Participation.* June 1989.

17   Usilaner, Brian; and Leitch, John. "Miles to Go...or Unity at Last," *Journal for Quality and Participation.* June 1989.

CHAPTER TWO

49   Stinnett, Robin Salem. "Quality Circles/ Quality of Worklife: An Innovation in Organizational Development," unpublished manuscript. March 1983.

50   Likert, Rensis. *New Patterns of Management.* New York: McGraw-Hill. 1961.

52   Sproul, R.C. *Stronger than Steel.* Pittsburgh, PA: W.T. Alderson. 1981.

CHAPTER THREE

81   Mohrman, S.A.; and Mohrman, Jr., A.M. "Employee Involvement in Declining Organizations," *Human Resource Management*

Magazine. March 1984.

CHAPTER FOUR

101   Lewin, Kurt. "Group Decision and Social
      Change," *Readings in Social Psychology,*
      3rd edition. Edited by E.E. Maccoby, E.C.
      Hartley. New York: Holt, Rinehart &
      Winston. 1958.

107   Dixon, Roger A., and John T. Hall. "Cyber-
      netic Sessions: A Technique for Gathering
      Ideas," *The 1974 Annual Handbook for
      Group Facilitators.* San Diego: University
      Associates. 1974.

CHAPTER SIX

157   Gordon, Thomas. *Leader Effectiveness Train-
      ing: The No-Lose Way to Release the Produc-
      tive Potential of People.* New York: G.P.
      Putnam's Sons. 1977.

CHAPTER SEVEN

165   Peters, Tom; and Austin, Nancy. *A Passion
      for Excellence.* New York: Random House
      Inc. 1985.

172   Pinchot III, Gifford. *Intrapreneuring: Why You
      Don't Have to Leave the Corporation to Be-
      come an Entrepreneur.* New York: Harper
      & Row, Publishers. 1985.

Index

A

Association for Quality and
  Participation 34
attitude survey 26
attitude surveys **156 - 158**

B

brainstorm 107
brainstorming 28 - 29, 107,
  114, 120, 133
bridge team 28 - 30, 34, **89 -
  93**, 97, 133, 136, 142, 158
business-within-a-business
  vi, 77

C

change, model of 101
change agent 76, 79, 89, 104,
  106, 109, 124
change agents 78 - 79, 83,
  88, 90, 163, 173
churn 81
coaches 39
code of conduct 119, **121 -
  122**, 174
commitment 21, 30, 63, 79,
  86 - 88, 102, 104, 109, 112
  - 113, 117, 125, 128, 161,
  170 - 171, 173 - 174
commitments 55
committed 86, 102, 170, 173
communication 48, 126
communication skill 157
communication skills 33,

118, 123, 125, 156
conflict 33 - 34, 95 - 96, 99,
  115, 123 - 124, 126, 174
conflicts 28, 31, 124, 153,
  160
consultant 119
consultants 39, 78, 173, 175
core group 33, 76, **84 - 89**,
  108 - 109, 114 - 116, 120,
  128, 156 - 157, 173
cost controls 48
cost reduction 12, 38
credibility 140 - 141
credo 21
  Also see manifesto
customer 12 - 14, 63, 151 -
  153, 165, 171, 177
customer satisfaction 14
customers 10, 151, 153, 165
cybernetic session 107, 114 -
  115

E

employee involvement (EI) 17
  - 18, 26 - 28, 36, 38 - 39,
  44, 47, 49, 51 - 52, 56 - 59,
  61 - 62, 64, 67 - 69, 74 - 75,
  78, 80 - 87, 90 - 91, 93,
  102, 104, 106 - 107, 109 -
  114, 116, 118, 120, 123,
  125, 127 - 131, 133, 140 -
  143, 155 - 156, 158, 160,
  162 - 167, 170, 172
employee involvement teams
  (EIT) 28, 98, 111 - 113,
  116 - 118, 124, 141, 162,

ABOUT THE AUTHORS

RUSSELL G. HANSON

Russell Hanson is president of TransTech, a consulting firm specializing in the management of organizational and technological change. Previously, he spent fourteen years with Honeywell Information Systems in Phoenix, Arizona. During this time, Mr. Hanson held positions in manufacturing engineering, production control, and operations management before becoming an internal organizational development consultant and forming the nucleus of Honeywell's Total Employee Involvement effort. He later became manager of Organizational Development for the Phoenix division. Prior to forming his own company in 1986, Mr. Hanson developed a set of consulting services to help Honeywell customers manage the human impact of technology change within their organizations.

Mr. Hanson holds a Master's degree in Industrial and Management Systems Engineering from Arizona State University. His professional affiliations include memberships in the Institute of Industrial Engineers, International Association of Quality Circles, and the Association for Quality and Participation.

WILLIAM D. STINNETT, PH.D.

Following four years as Assistant Professor at the Department of Communications at Arizona State University, Dr. Stinnett accepted a position at Honeywell in 1980. With co-author Russ Hanson and Bill Van Horn, he developed and implemented Total Employee Involvement at several Honeywell locations. In 1985, he established the Human Productivity Center, a consulting and training business devoted to assisting companies achieve their goals through employees involvement. As president of the Human Productivity Center, Dr. Stinnett has served corporations from many industries, including electronics, defense, oil refining, manufacturing, utilities, and government. Among his clients are Motorola, Intel, Florida Power & Light, and Procter & Gamble.

Dr. Stinnett's education includes a B.A. from Marshall University in Speech and Theatre, an M.A. in Interpersonal Communication from Ohio University, and a Ph.D. in Communication from the University of Florida.

TOGETHER, Mr. Hanson and Dr. Stinnett helped develop the fundamental concepts outlined in this book. During their work with Honeywell in the early 1980s, they initiated a Total Employee Involvement effort that resulted in a 330 percent increase in productivity over an eight month period, a 54 percent reduction in product cost, a first-time yield increase from 60 percent to 95 percent, and a $4 million first-year savings. Their model has been successfully applied in numerous other organizations with similar results.

CORPORATE MADNESS
is your roadmap to success!
Order your copy today.

❏ **YES!** I want to build a winning team!

Name _____

Company _____

Title _____

Address _____

City, State & Zip _____

Phone O: _____

Send $17.95 for each book you wish to order. Add $1.75 for postage and handling on the first book, .50 for each additional book. Allow 4-6 weeks for delivery. Make checks payable and send your orders to **Leadership Press, 124 W. Orion, Suite F-10, Tempe Arizona 85283.**

Please send me _____ **books at $17.95 each** .... _____

Postage and handling .... _____

Tax (Arizona residents add .90 per book) .... _____

TOTAL amount enclosed .... _____

CREDIT CARD ORDERS:

VISA ❏   MASTERCARD ❏   AMERICAN EXPRESS ❏

Card #

Expiration Date: _____ Signature: _____

Or order by phone! 1-800-729-9494

——————————————— ⅃⎸P ———————————————

Leadership Press books are available at special quantity discounts for sales promotions, premiums, or educational uses. Special books, book excerpts, and other materials can also be created to meet specific needs. For more information, please contact our Special Projects Coordinator, Leadership Press, 124 W. Orion, Suite F-10, Tempe AZ 85283; (602) 730-1752.

CORPORATE MADNESS
is your roadmap to success!
Order your copy today.

❏ **YES!** I want to build a winning team!

Name _____

Company _____

Title _____

Address _____

City, State & Zip_____

Phone O: _____

Send $17.95 for each book you wish to order. Add $1.75 for postage and handling on the first book, .50 for each additional book. Allow 4-6 weeks for delivery. Make checks payable and send your orders to **Leadership Press, 124 W. Orion, Suite F-10, Tempe Arizona 85283.**

Please send me _____ **books at $17.95 each** . . . . _____

Postage and handling . . . . _____

Tax (Arizona residents add .90 per book) . . . . _____

TOTAL amount enclosed . . . . _____

CREDIT CARD ORDERS:

VISA ❏   MASTERCARD ❏   AMERICAN EXPRESS ❏

Card # | | | | | | | | | | | | | | | | | | | |

Expiration Date:_____ Signature:_____

Or order by phone! 1-800-729-9494

Leadership Press books are available at special quantity discounts for sales promotions, premiums, or educational uses. Special books, book excerpts, and other materials can also be created to meet specific needs. For more information, please contact our Special Projects Coordinator, Leadership Press, 124 W. Orion, Suite F-10, Tempe AZ 85283; (602) 730-1752.